FROM THE FOOTPLATE

ELIZABETHAN

Edinburgh Waverley to Lon

C000155316

IAN ALLAN
Publishing

FROM THE FOOTPLATE
ELIZABETHAN
Edinburgh Waverley to London King's Cross

STEPHEN AUSTIN

First published 1993

ISBN 0 7110 2152 X

© Ian Allan Ltd 1993

Published by Ian Allan Ltd, Shepperton, Surrey; and printed by Ian Allan Printing Ltd at their works at Coombelands in Runnymede, England.

Previous page:
Farthest and fastest; the up 'Elizabethan' passing Penmanshiel Cottage on Cockburnspath Bank on 1 July 1957. The LNER postwar train in maroon livery hauled by *Mallard*, beautifully turned out down to her polished buffers.
H. K. Harman

Front cover:
The most famous 'A4' of them all. No 60022 *Mallard* departs from Edinburgh Waverley with the southbound 'Elizabethan'.
J. T. Inglis/Colour-Rail

Contents

Preface

This monograph is not intended to be a technical treatise on the East Coast route, its history or its motive power. It is offered to the reader who knows a little of our railways and has heard that, in their past, they were more ramified than in their present; who has heard that men used to run trains non-stop between London and Edinburgh; and who would like a general summary of how that amazing feat was achieved. (Anyone who would accuse the writer of hyperbole in describing the running of steam trains in those terms is recommended to try it for themselves).

Sources
The full story of the non-stop trains is told by A. J. Mullay in *Non-Stop!*, and the engine *Mallard* has her book *Mallard the Record-Breaker* by M. Rutherford. Other essential sources include the LNER's *From Either Side, The Coronation* by C. J. Allen, *The First Railway Across the Border* by G. Dow, *Yeadon's Register of LNER Locomotives*, the David & Charles *Regional History of the Railways of Great Britain*, *Kings Cross* by C. Hawkins, *Rail Centres: Doncaster* by S. Batty, *Enginemen Elite* by Norman MacKillop, the columns of the *Railway Magazine*, and of course the records held in those fine institutions the Public Record Office and the Scottish Record Office.

Acknowledgements
I would like to record special thanks to Keith Jackson, David Wilkinson and the A4 Locomotive Society, Richard Gibbon and the National Railway Museum, Messrs. P. Townend, H. K. Harman, T. C. Robbins, J. Cameron, I. S. Carr, Mrs A. Hatherill and Miss J. Mackenzie.

Regular non-stop running between London and Edinburgh finished on 9 September 1961. The up train was hauled by *Union of South Africa*, which is now owned by Mr John Cameron and based in Scotland as she has been all her life. The down run was made by *Mallard*, now usually on display in the National Railway Museum, York, whence she makes the occasional excursion. A third 'A4' class engine, *Sir Nigel Gresley*, is operated by the A4 Locomotive Society and leads a roving life, touring the country, and is probably the most widely known of the three. The traveller who would repeat the experience of being sat in a train for 6½hrs will have to forgo it in the 1990s, for great as the achievements of railway restoration are, one thing no-one can yet do is pick up water at speed. However, on the Llangollen Railway one can sample one of the coaches built for the service, LNER Lounge Buffet Car No 1706.

In these pages the word 'engine' is used to mean a steam railway locomotive engine; and the engine we describe is referred to as 'she', inanimate machine or no. I consider that to do otherwise is to insult the men who created, operated and maintained her and who keep her for posterity.

At the end of this account you may sit back and feel thankful that what is described is all in the past. Nowadays we have different ideas on what are worthwhile goals in life and what things are enjoyable or allowable to do. I would just raise the question, though: did anything of value get thrown out along with the toil and sweat, noise and dirt, smoke and steam? If this account gives you reason to ponder that question, it will have served its purpose.

Introduction

If you have a liking for maps and a sense of place, you may be able to see, even as you sit here, the shape of Britain spread before you, with the cities of London and Edinburgh, and all the hills and valleys, rivers and towns which separate them. If you have a feel for history, you may also be able to visualise the passage of the years like a scale or graph, on which you can alight at any point you choose. For instance, Cockenzie by the Firth of Forth in 1722, there to find coals from the mines of Newbattle being drawn by horses down a new 'railway'. Or a town-house in York in 1842, and an ambitious shopkeeper saying 'Mak' all t'railways come to York'. Or the flood plain of the Yorkshire Ouse in 1980, with a great white strip being laid firm and level across the countryside.

My choice now is to take you to the year 1955, to a summer morning in Princes Street, Edinburgh. There is no mistaking the location, for nowhere else can you stand on a city street and view the roof-top of the adjoining railway station. When you walk down the long steps between the Waverley Market and the North British Hotel, you hear a sound, amid all the many sounds, which is also quite unmistakable. It is a sort of dry rasping, not so high as a hiss nor so deep as to be a roar. It comes from a very special steam locomotive, of the class designated 'A4', which is ready to haul a unique train. Currently known as the 'Elizabethan' it has had other titles since its inception, but in railway households all along the East Coast route it is the 'Non-Stop'.

This is a journey from Edinburgh Waverley to London King's Cross on the longest non-stop passenger train service in the world. We are riding with the engine crews: two of them, as they change over half-way through whilst at speed, something which is done nowhere else. It is done daily from 27 June to 9 September.

When you recall what a tiny scrap of land Britain is, it is astonishing that it holds this particular record, but such is true provided that we are clear as to what we mean. It is of course possible to travel 10 times as far without a change of carriage in other parts of the world, but with many pauses on the way.

In 1943 the Atchison, Topeka & Santa Fe Railroad was running steam engines through between Los Angeles and Kansas City, a distance of 1,788 miles, which took about 45hrs and was an impressive feat, but again there were numerous stops. The absolute non-stop record is, naturally, claimed in America; 1,017 miles from Chicago to Denver run on 23 October 1936 by a diesel train. However, the longest journey without a scheduled stop on a regular train available to fare-paying passengers is that between London and Edinburgh.

To be fair, there are harder long-distance jobs even in this country. The prewar 'Coronation' was hauled the same distance by one engine, with only a couple of brief halts which could hardly be said to be any easement, and took only six hours. At present the 'Duchess' class engines on the West Coast route work through between London and Glasgow with but a momentary stop at Carlisle to change crews, and they do it all the year round, with a heavier load, on a more difficult road. However, by a mixture of panache, publicity and star quality, the 'Elizabethan' has come to be regarded as the ultimate steam train, so this must be the acme of footplate rides. Before embarking on it, we will look briefly at how it came into being.

Its origin lay in the intense rivalry between the East Coast and West Coast partnerships, which culminated in the races from London to Aberdeen in the summer of 1895. The excesses of that event led to a gentlemen's agreement that no train would take less than 8¼hrs between London and Glasgow or Edinburgh. The focus of competition then shifted to passenger comfort, and the Great Northern, North Eastern and North British companies' pooled carriages, called the East Coast Joint Stock, became opulent in the extreme. Meanwhile, in 1904, the Great Western Railway began a new record non-stop service between London and Plymouth, and made sure everyone heard about it. After 20 years of non-stop publicity the London & North Eastern Railway, as the East Coast companies had become, decided to do something about it (after all, their own King's Cross-Grantham route had been the record holder in its day), so in 1927 the premier Scottish express, the 'Flying Scotsman' ran through to Newcastle, 268 miles. The rival London, Midland & Scottish Railway promptly capped that with 299 miles to Carlisle, so the LNER Board and their strongly competitive Chief Mechanical Engineer, H. N. Gresley, resolved on a decisive leap: to Edinburgh, 392 miles 69 chains. The 'Flying Scotsman' skipped its Newcastle stop from 1 May 1928 in a blaze of advertisement which carefully omitted to mention that the 8¼hr cartel was still in effect. It must have been pretty tedious, trundling along at a speed comparable to that of a fast goods train, but patrons were treated to new heights of luxury; this was the train with the Powder Room, Hairdresser and on-board Wireless. It went so far that the enthusiast press, which in those days never criticised the railways, actually published letters of dissent from disgruntled enginemen who were raising ever more steam to shift around grandiose mobile restaurants with ever fewer travellers to the ton. In 1932 came another change; speed was once more on the agenda, culminating in the lightweight coaches and 71mph schedule of the 'Coronation'. In this period the LNER commissioned artist Eric Gill to give it a new go-faster image, for which he designed the Gill Sans lettering. It also engaged Sissons Paints on a scheme of redecoration and lineside garden planting, and more seriously embarked on the immense programme of track modernisation and electric signalling which shaped the main line as we know it today.

During the war, of course speed and luxury went out with the lights, and in 1955 we are still recovering from that era. When the 'Non-Stop' was revived in 1949 it was called the 'Capitals Limited' and was an addition to the timetable, leaving the 'Flying Scotsman' to call at Newcastle. New train sets were built, not as grand as the prewar ones but equipped with pressure-ventilation and including a kitchen, buffet, first and third-class dining car and a full-length baggage van. In 1953 the title was changed to the 'Elizabethan' in accordance with the patriotic fervour of that summer, and the time is now down to 6½hrs. The load is limited to 11 vehicles with a tare weight of around 400 tons. The postwar LNER sets are still used, repainted into carmine and cream livery, but sometimes the catering vehicles are ordinary prewar stock, and sometimes new BR standard coaches are seen. However, in the timetable there is, even now, an echo of the 1930s in the announcement that the train carries Refreshment Cars, Buffet Car and Ladies Retiring Rooms with Attendants.

Being a record holder may attract publicity, but it is reasonable to ask whether the complications of the 'Non-Stop' are justified in financial terms, especially when it is done with tax-payers' money. The official answer has always been that, partly, the publicity attracts business, and, mainly, it is worth running a train through to Edinburgh as long as it can be filled with passengers who are travelling that far or farther, and to whom intermediate stops are a waste of time and money. There is no doubt that stopping a train and accelerating it up to speed again costs a lot, but where there are major stations which have to be negotiated at speeds as low as 15mph even when not stopping, that argument sounds a trifle stretched. There may be some special pleading here, but then what price do you put on prestige?

Beyond the business arguments, there is another adequate reason for running this train: for fun. All animals play, and if you deny us the right to use the resources we have so laboriously obtained in order to have fun, you have denied the whole of art, sport and home comforts, and set us below the level of the beasts. And the 'Non-Stop' is essentially fun. If you do not enter into the spirit of the attempt not to stop, the special arrangements for it, such as changing crews in motion, become pointless. Directors might frown at footplatemen having a two-day outing in which they are only working the train for seven hours, but have they not as much right to it as the directors have to an occasional business lunch? For the railway company to indulge in something frivolous is as allowable as the Durham Miners' Gala or the Blaydon Races.

So let us now accept the 'Elizabethan' as it is, and go out and do it.

The Power

The 'Non-Stop' is normally hauled by a Class A4 Gresley Pacific: that is, an engine of the 4-6-2 wheel arrangement built to the designs of Sir Nigel Gresley. ('Pacific' is an American nickname applied to any 4-6-2 engine.) The series started with the Class A1 of 1922; though powerful, they were not economical enough on coal and water for long-distance running, and the design was considerably modified in consultation with the then non-stop experts, the Great Western Railway, before the distance race began in 1927. Class A4 appeared in 1935 as part of a totally new product: a purpose-built high-speed train. In order to cruise at up to 90mph the design was further modified with a higher boiler pressure and

9in diameter piston valves, and they were the first British engines in which the steam pipes and ports were smoothed on the inside. A more visible feature was an overall streamlined casing. Although intended to work the lightweight 'Silver Jubilee', 'Coronation' and 'West Riding' trains, the 'A4s' were also highly capable on ordinary passenger work — eg, No 4490 *Empire of India* once lifted a 17-coach, 635-ton express over Stoke summit at 48mph, and the first of the class, No 2509 *Silver Link*, hauled 25 coaches from King's Cross to Newcastle on 5 April 1940 — and 35 were built.

Today they are the only surviving streamlined engines. The casing is claimed to save 97hp when running at 80mph, so after two hours at that speed we may expect to have shovelled ¼ton less coal than on an unclad engine, which is not to be despised. The appearance of the sloping front is not to everyone's taste, and it is an inconvenience in servicing, as it has to be opened up to gain access to the smokebox. The unique aerofoil-shaped gangway, said to have been a sudden inspiration on the part of Gresley's assistant O. V. S. Bulleid while the first engine was being assembled, is an aesthetic master-stroke, but less easy to walk on than a flat one. The casing also adds a resonance of its own to the noises of the engine, making it distinguishable by sound as much as by sight.

A speciality of Gresley engines is their arrangement with three cylinders but only two sets of valve motion. The valve for the middle cylinder is actuated by two rocking arms driven by the outside valve spindles, a linkage called, after the proportions of one of them, the 'two to one lever'. It looks a very elegant piece of geom-

Left:
The 'A4' footplate: *Dominion of Canada*, photographed when new in 1937. The Flaman speed recorder is under the right-hand seat. The most important items are the vacuum brake ejector, above the left-hand seat, and the injectors poking out under the framing at the bottom, live steam on the left, exhaust on the right. The firehole is obscured by hinged heat-shield plates.
British Railways

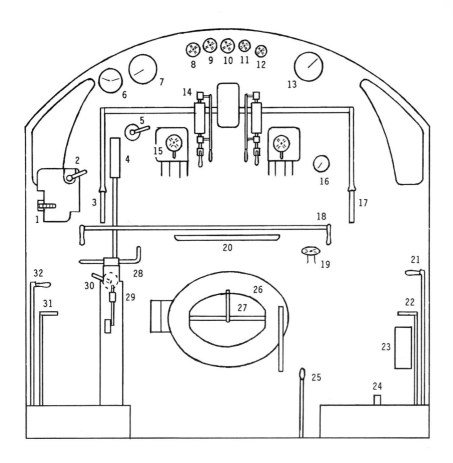

Cab Controls, A4 Class Engine

1   Large ejector & brake valve
2   Small ejector
3   Regulator
4   Reverser scale
5   Blower
6   Duplex vacuum gauge
7   Steam chest pressure gauge
Steam stop valves:
    8 Steam sanding
    9 Brake ejector
    10 Blower
    11 Pressure gauge
    12 Train heat
13 Boiler pressure gauge
14 Boiler water gauges
15 Combined injector steam valves
                    & clacks
16 Train heat gauge

17 Duplicate regulator handle
18 Whistle
19 Coal watering tap
20 Tea-tray
21 Cylinder cocks
22 Water regulator ∘
        (exhaust injector)
23 Flaman recorder
24 Drop grate screw
25 Damper
26 Firedoor
27 Firedoor flap
28 Reverser
29 Reverser lock
30 Steam sand
31 Water regulator
        (live injector)
32 Gravity sand

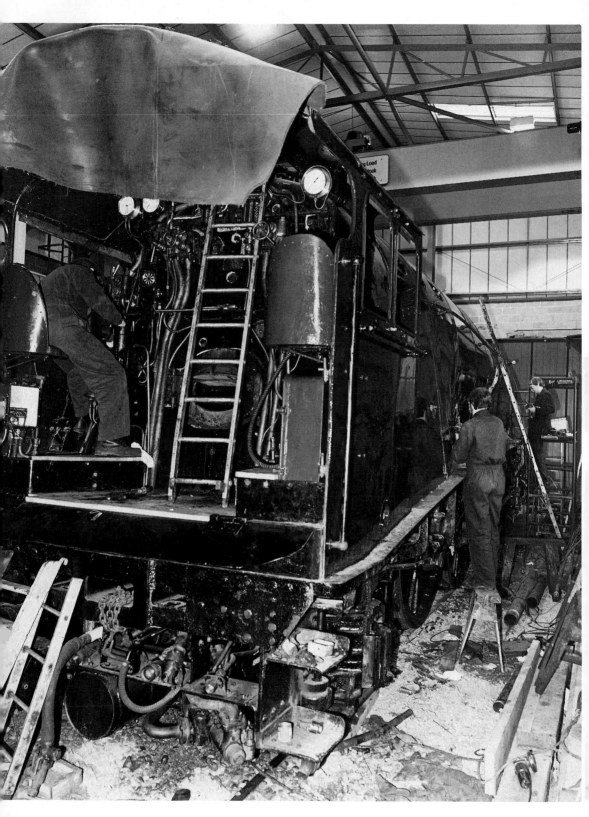

Left:

A present-day 'A4' cab, *Union of South Africa*, under overhaul in the Severn Valley Railway works at Bridgnorth in 1990. The principal additions are AWS equipment: relay unit under the driver's seat, battery box under the fireman's seat and two vacuum reservoirs under the framing. Behind the ladder is the firehole with main door closed and flap open, as it is for normal firing.
K. J. C. Jackson

Bottom:

Driver's Seat on *Sir Nigel Gresley*. On this engine the cut-off indicator has been marked in yellow paint down behind the reverser, because the proper scale is out of sight of anyone standing across the cab. Above the reverser handle is a notice instructing you to coast in 25% when above 25mph.
SHA

Right:

Fireman's Seat. Leaning by the window are a firing shovel and a 'T' handle for opening the 'drop grate' — a hinged section of firebars.
SHA

Left:
Those who prefer the traditional front view will not like this, but it adds variety to the scene. In our view it is the only example of streamlining on a steam engine to be at all acceptable aesthetically.
SHA

Right:
A '2-1' valve lever. This one is from another Gresley engine, *The Great Marquess*, and was seen at Bridgnorth, Severn Valley Railway. When installed it occupies the whole width of the front of the engine.
SHA

Below and below right:
In these enlightened times everyone is allowed to see what an 'A4' looks like in the nude. These two pictures show the boiler of the preserved *Sir Nigel Gresley* in June 1992, undergoing a steam test and being refitted to the engine. The latter shows how the smokebox fits over the block containing the middle cylinder, and on that, showing as two black squares, are the twin exhaust steam nozzles of the Kylchap double chimney.
K. J. C. Jackson

Above:
Tender front, driver's side. The vertical shaft is the water gauge. A 'NOT TO BE MOVED' sign is tucked behind the curved pipe which acts as an overflow warning when filling the tank. Stacked where the funnel used to be are wood blocks used as wheel scotches. On this *Sir Nigel Gresley's* tender, the water scoop was removed years ago; the handle was in front of the shelf. The small handle is a tap for a water pipe to the engine. At the top are fire-irons in their stowage.
SHA

Right:
Tender front, fireman's side: the corridor door and, right, handbrake handle and another water tap.
SHA

Above:
Interior of tender corridor of 'A4' No 4498 *Sir Nigel Gresley.*
SHA

etry, but in practice it is difficult to set it up to give the engine an even exhaust beat and the result is often a pronounced waltz-time from the chimney.

Coupled behind the engine is the device that makes the 'Non-Stop' possible – the corridor tender. Twenty-four of these are in use and are the only ones of their kind in the world. The corridor is a simple steel tunnel 5ft high and 18in wide, running along the right-hand side, with a standard coach vestibule connection at the

Above:
A rear view of *Union of South Africa* showing the tender corridor connector. This photograph was taken at Aberdeen Ferryhill, where several of these engines made their last runs in British Railways service.
J. B. Cameron

back. Despite the space it takes up, the same coal and water capacity as in the non-corridor version is obtained by building the tender up to the permitted limits of height and width, which means that the engine crew have no rear view unless they stick their heads outside the loading gauge.

There is another special feature on the 'A4' class: an amazingly poignant whistle. It was the LMSR, which did everything by committee, that decided that a low-pitched sound was more pleasing to the ear and therefore adopted an organ-pipe. But a locomotive whistle is not meant to be nice to listen to, it is meant to attract attention, and the LNER standard type, sounding like a suffering pig, is undoubtedly effective for that. For the introduction of a sound both attention-getting and musical, we have to thank the engine about which this book should have been written, *Cock O'the North*. She was given a Canadian whistle by the owners of the Romney,

15

Hythe & Dymchurch Railway, and someone persuaded the LNER Board to purchase something similar for the 'Silver Jubilee'. It is an organ-pipe type, but it contains three pipes tuned in harmony and is consequently termed a chime whistle. It does not always sound as it should, but when tuned correctly it goes straight through your ears to your soul and raises echoes in part of your psyche you usually find it more comfortable to forget. There is no fathoming what prompted commercially-minded men to put so magical a device on so prosaic a thing as a railway engine; perhaps it meant nothing to them. The vast majority of people think nothing of it, or of any other aspect of trains. But if you have any romance left in you, listen to it. Go up to St Anthony's Chapel on the side of Arthur's Seat and listen to it faint above the din of the city as the engine arrives in Waverley; clear between you and Calton Hill as she passes Holyrood; wafting back from the east to say that the 'Eliza-bethan' is on its way. Listen to it, for I can't describe it.

As a final comment on streamlining, when big engines with very short chimneys appeared on our railways, a newspaper invited its readers to compose poems lamenting the diminution of that appendage. The results showed that in the public mind an engine without a tall chimney was clearly not driven by steam!

Below:
'A4' tête-à-tête at York, 5 May 1988. This shows the prewar casing below gangway level which was reinstated on *Mallard* when she was preserved. On *Sir Nigel Gresley* can be seen the valve spindle guides and one end of the '2-1' lever. On both engines, above the back of the leading wheel, is the hole where you put a handle to open up the 'cod's mouth'.
K. J. C. Jackson

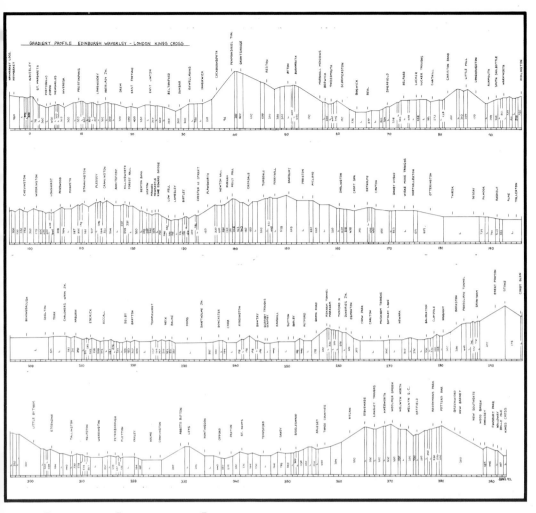

Technical Details

Overall length:	71ft 5in
height:	13ft 1in
width:	9ft
Weight: engine	empty 93 tons, full 103 tons
tender	empty 34 tons, full 65 tons
Firegrate area:	41¼sq.ft.
Heating surface area:	3,325sq.ft.
Boiler diameter:	6ft 5in
Boiler tube length:	17ft 11in
Boiler pressure:	250lb/sq in
Cylinder bore:	18½in (three)
Piston stroke:	26in
Valve diameter:	9in
Valve travel:	6⅝in
Coupled wheel diameter:	6ft 8in
Brakes:	Vacuum on engine and tender
Tender coal capacity:	9 tons
Tender water capacity:	5,000gal

The Route

The oldest part of the East Coast line is from Parkhead, Darlington, to Croft, which is on the alignment of a branch of the Stockton & Darlington Railway opened in 1829. This minor connection with the first public railway to use steam locomotives has served as the basis for the publicity department's claim that this is 'the world's oldest main line'. The last link to be inserted was the King Edward Bridge, in 1906 — before then all trains had to cross the Tyne by the High Level Bridge and reverse in Newcastle station. The first trains to reach York from London did so via Rugby, in 1840, using George Hudson's York & North Midland Railway. By the summer of 1844 there was a through service from the Thames to the Tyne via Darlington, Penshaw, Washington and Boldon. In 1846 the North British Railway opened from Edinburgh to Berwick, followed by the Newcastle & Berwick a year later, and the chain was completed by the High Level Bridge and the Royal Border Bridge over the Tweed, both products of the genius of Robert Stephenson. The direct route between London and York resulted largely from the energy of Edmund Denison, MP for Doncaster, whose Great Northern Railway was pushed through in the teeth of entrenched opposition, particularly from the Hudson empire, and was completed in 1852. The present (1955) main lines from Doncaster to York through Selby and from Ferryhill to Durham did not come into use until 1872.

It cannot be denied that much of the country on the southern half of the route is flat and affords little of obvious interest from the carriage windows. This enabled the engineers to lay their railways out for speed, and the Great North of England from York to Darlington, virtually straight and level, was for many years the busiest in Europe and carried the fastest trains. These racing grounds suffered during the war when the maintenance of track for high speeds became an unaffordable luxury, and even now, although the overall speed ceiling is 90mph, most of the line south of Peterborough carries limits of 85mph or less. In Northumberland and Durham the main line cuts across numerous river valleys, entailing major engineering features and sharp curves, and there is the added threat of subsidence in an area which has been mined for over 350 years, so the limit is 80mph between Darlington and Durham, 75mph between Newton Hall and Newcastle, with numerous slower sections. North of Newcastle, where the route really is on the East Coast, 90mph is permitted, but there are stiffer gradients, particularly on the sections where it snakes through the eastern end of the Lammermuir Hills. Here southbound trains face the only severe incline on the line, 4½ miles at 1 in 96. It is against these constraints that the mile-a-minute schedule of the 'Non-Stop' should be appreciated.

Keeping Time

The public timetable only advertises two times: Depart 9.45am, Arrive 4.15pm. However, for the crew it is not a case of 'Cheerio, see you in London', they have a detailed schedule to follow. To achieve the start-to-stop average speed of 60.4mph needs fast running, but all-out thrashing is definitely out. Any fool can go faster by using more fuel and making more noise; that is not good driving, on the railway or on the road either. Going too hard erodes the profit from the fares to no purpose, and of course running out of fuel or getting stopped because you are ahead of time destroys the principal objective of the run.

In practice the 'A4s' have plenty in hand on this job and it is quite usual to cut up to 20 min off the running time in retrieving traffic delays. Coal is not normally a problem; at 40lb a mile we would use just over seven tons, at 45lb a mile eight tons, and with nicely sized South Yorkshire coal and careful stacking it is possible to get nearly 11 tons on the tender. Water is another matter, for we will need about 13,000gal, and this is where the water troughs come in. From Edinburgh to the first trough at Lucker is 73 miles. By then we will be down to about half the tank-full, and should pick up some 2,000gal. At Wiske Moor, 98 miles on, the tender will be less than a quarter full and a good pick-up is essential, for the next 76 miles to Scrooby will take us down to 800gal or so. If anything goes wrong here a stop to fill up at a station water column will be inevitable. The closely-spaced troughs of Scrooby and Trent (or Muskham) are both needed to restore our supply to about 4,000gal, but after that it is plain sailing as Werrington and Langley will replace what we use, and we should still have 3-4,000gal aboard when we reach King's Cross. Water is indeed the critical part of the whole operation, and as late as the spring of 1955 the tender water scoops were modified to dig deeper into the troughs.

It is vital all the time to avoid wasting water by unnecessarily harsh driving or blowing off at the safety valves, and the exhaust steam injector, which uses steam that would otherwise go up the chimney to feed water into the boiler, and can save up to 10% of water consumption, must be in good order.

'THE ELIZABETHAN'
Schedule DOWN Train,
Summer 1955 timetable

Miles.
chains

0	King's Cross	dep 9.30am
10.10	Greenwood	9.45
17.54	Hatfield	9.53
31.64	Hitchin	10.6
58.70	Huntingdon North	10.28
76.29	Peterborough North	10.44½
79.40	Werrington Jn	10.49½
88.52	Essendine	10.57½
105.40	Grantham	11.13½
109.56	Barkston South Jn	11.17
120.68	Newark	11.26
139.29	Retford	11.43
155.77	Doncaster	12.00
159.33	Shaftholme Jn	12.5pm
174.25	Selby	12.18
188.11	York	12.33
189.60	Skelton	12.36
199.25	Alne	12.44½
210.27	Thirsk	12.54½
218.07	Northallerton	1.1½
227.06	Eryholme	1.8½
232.21	Darlington	1.13
245.09	Ferryhill	1.25
254.24	Durham	1.34½
267.59	King Edward Bridge	1.49½
268.27	Newcastle on Tyne	1.51½
284.77	Morpeth	2.11½
303.16	Alnmouth	2.28½
319.79	Belford	2.44½
335.27	Berwick upon Tweed	2.59
336.29	Marshall Meadows	3.01
346.47	Reston	3.12
351.49	Grantshouse	3.18
363.49	Dunbar	3.29
375.09	Drem	3.39
386.57	Monktonhall Jn	3.50
389.56	Portobello	3.54
392.69	Waverley	arr 4.0

2

THE 'ELIZABETHAN'
Schedule UP Train Summer 1955 timetable

miles.chains			average speed mph	restrictions mph
–	Aberdeen	dep 5.47		
–	Dundee Tay Bridge	dep 7.42		
–	Waverley	arr 9.29		
0	Waverley	dep 9.45 am		
3.13	Portobello	9.50	40	40/60
6.12	Monktonhall Jn	9.55	36	60
17.60	Drem	10.6	63	90
29.20	Dunbar	10.16	69	90/60
41.20	Grantshouse	10.30	51	70/90
46.22	Reston	10.35	60	90
56.40	Marshall Meadows	10.44	68	90
57.42	Berwick upon Tweed	10.46	30	60/30
72.70	Belford	11.0½	64	50/90
89.53	Alnmouth	11.16	65	90
107.72	Morpeth	11.33	65	90/70
124.42	Newcastle on Tyne	11.51	55	90/75/45
125.10	King Edward Bridge	11.53	18	20
138.45	Durham	12.7 pm	58	50/75/65/30
147.60	Ferryhill	12.17½	52	50/80
160.48	Darlington	12.29½	64	80
165.63	Eryholme	12.34	69	80
174.62	Northallerton	12.41½	72	90
182.42	Thirsk	12.48	72	90
193.44	Alne	12.57	74	90
203.09	Skelton	1.4½	76	90
204.58	York	1.7½	32	50/25
218.44	Selby	1.22½	55	90/50
233.36	Shaftholme Jn	1.38½	56	90
236.72	Doncaster	1.43	46	60
253.40	Retford G.N.	2.0½	57	80
272.01	Newark Northgate	2.17	67	80
283.13	Barkston South Jn	2.26½	70	85
287.29	Grantham	2.30½	63	85
304.17	Essendine	2.44	75	90
313.29	Werrington Jn	2.51	73	90
316.40	Peterborough North	2.55½	42	60/20
333.79	Huntingdon North	3.13	60	85/65
361.05	Hitchin	3.36½	72	85/90
367.76	Knebworth	3.43	64	85
375.15	Hatfield	3.50	53	70
380.12	Potters Bar	3.56	50	60
390.28	Finsbury Park	4.10	44	60
392.69	King's Cross	arr 4.15	30	40
–	King's Cross	dep 4.50		
–	Hornsey C. S.	arr 7.0		

Above and below:
Portraits of the up and down 'Elizabethans', both on 15 August 1960 and both near Meadowfield, south of Durham city. The northbound train, hauled by the 'A4' *Falcon*, is slowing for the 30mph restriction through the town, and the southbound, hauled by *Gannet*, is gathering speed. The latter shows how the graceful curved side gangway on the 'A4s' was marred on the left-hand side by a rather clumsily-applied conduit, which carries an electric cable to the Automatic Warning System receiver at the front of the engine. *Both I. S. Carr*

Organisation

Working the 'Non-Stop' demands a high level of professionalism from all the railwaymen involved. It is the highest-paid footplate job in the country, for all that it looks to the layman like an easy number — 3¼hrs running, then nothing until another 3¼hrs the following day, with a lodging allowance and free lunches in it. But like all professionals at the peak of their career, the enginemen are paid not just for what they do but for what they know and what they have done to reach this responsible position. Knowledge of the steam engine, which like all simple tools places great reliance on the skill of the user, is only part of it. The top-link driver knows every yard of the road literally with his eyes shut, knows the operating rules and the local regulations for each station and siding, and above all he knows the function of every signal.

It is important to realise that no driver ever moves an engine just on his own initiative. He always obeys instructions, given either by hand signals or by the fixed lineside signals. Although the latter are standardised, the precise actions permitted or prohibited by them must inevitably depend on the location, so he must learn them all individually. For instance, at Acklington, the up home signal No 33 has an extra colour light signal, No R33, below it on the post. This is normally out, but is switched on to show a red by the control at the adjoining airfield if they have an emergency, in which case trains must stop regardless of the aspects of the other signals. Whether it is a single signal like this or the array of arms or lights at a big junction, the enginemen must instantly read and understand their messages. Moreover, driving a train is one of the few jobs in which no error can be allowed. Mistakes made on this page can be rubbed out and corrected, but with 570 tons of train and 420 human souls covering 100ft or more in every second, there is no second chance; the driver must get it right all the way, without the smallest lapse in attention or judgement. In fact, 200 miles represents a pretty demanding day's work.

Many other people besides the enginemen have to do their jobs right, for the train would not go through non-stop, or at all, if the signalmen and controllers did not keep a multitude of other trains moving in their proper paths. They in turn rely on the men out on the line. At Sandy, the station is a bottleneck with only two tracks through the platforms. The 1.40pm New England-Ferme Park goods train runs through at about 3.13pm and shunts into the up sidings, whence it continues on the goods line at 3.25pm. The 10.50am New England-Hitchin pick-up goods train leaves Tempsford at 3.10pm and arrives in Sandy's goods yard at 3.23pm, by which time the 'Elizabethan' is passing Tempsford and will go through Sandy at about 3.26. If one of those goods trains were unduly tardy and did not clear the section in time, the result would be the 'Non-Stop', stopped.

To look further, there is the contribution of the shed staff. The 'A4s' are praised for their reliability (for in 1955 no time was recorded as lost by engine defects), but this is achieved with the aid of an amount of maintenance which would be unthinkable for, say, a diesel engine operator. At King's Cross Locomotive Depot they are supplied with a special oil with 25% rapeseed oil content. They also receive selected coal, although at Haymarket they have to take whatever comes from the hopper. At one time the 'Non-Stop' engine had its fire removed and its boiler refilled with clean water after every trip, although now this is only done on the weekly examination and washout. The middle connecting rod big-end is taken down and examined every 12,000 miles, and the '2-1' valve lever is stripped every 20,000 miles. The coupled wheel axleboxes have to be made to individual sizes to avoid the problem of their running hot, and the depot keeps spares for each engine in the stores. At both King's Cross and Haymarket most of the top-link engines are allocated to regular crews and do the same variety of work as their men, but early in each year the best engines are selected for the 'Non-Stop' season and put into a separate group. Every day, a standby engine is prepared at the same time as the booked engine, and is only released for other service after the train has departed. The depots at Tweedmouth, Gateshead, Darlington, York, Doncaster and Grantham each have to keep a large passenger engine ready to move out at a few minutes' notice, and on Saturdays these spare engines are positioned in the stations. All these provisions are considered justifiable to assure the dependability of service that people expect and deserve from our railways.

The 'Elizabethan' is unusual in that the duty worked by the men is similar to that of the engines and is devoted entirely to one train. The King's Cross crew work the southern half of each journey, out one day and home the next, while Haymarket men do the same from their end. Although there is no 'Non-Stop' at weekends, the same arrangement applies, because the outgoing men on Friday must get home on Saturday and the incoming men on Monday work outwards on Sunday. The trains used are the 9am King's Cross-Edinburgh and 9.45am Edinburgh-King's Cross on Saturday, and the 10am down and 10.50am up on Sunday, all of which stop at York and Newcastle so that there is no real need to change over on the move. A man can do any two-day stint, although it is usual to take a week at a time. Allocation to this top job is, officially at least, strictly according to seniority.

The engines work on a two-week cycle which is best explained by the diagram:

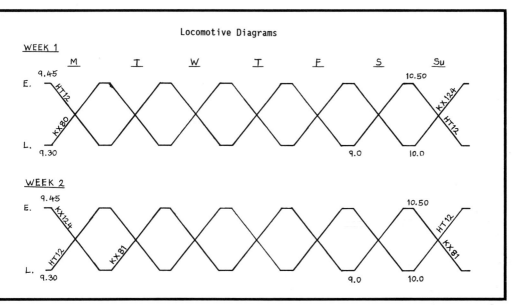

KX80, KX81 and KX124 are the King's Cross duty numbers and HT12 is the Haymarket duty. The Eastern Region also applies serial numbers to all the trains in the timetable: even numbers to down trains and odd numbers to up trains. The up 'Elizabethan' is No 67. The carriages forming the trains are kept together in sets and have numbered duties in the same way as the engines. Some are very complex: passengers on the evening service from Edinburgh to Corstorphine often find themselves in a main line set hauled by an express engine. The latter then retires to Haymarket shed while the coaches are left in the little station overnight to form a morning up service. Incidentally, all these numbers are quite unrelated to the stock numbers carried on the vehicles, a point productive of some confusion in the public mind, although not as much as that caused by names. To give an engine the same name as the most famous train, the 'Flying Scotsman', was the silliest choice the LNER board ever made, for they should have known that no journalist will ever be able to grasp the difference between the two.

Larkrise in Edinburgh

Before we start, it must be mentioned that this is an international train, for regardless of what politicians may think, the Scots are a nation, Scotland is a country and Edinburgh is its capital city. If you are an English traveller making the journey south, you may already, on arriving here, have encountered one or two culture shocks. Fortunately for you, Edinburgh is hardly in the true Scotland. You may think you have come a long way from London, but be reminded that the distance from here to the northwest corner of the country is comparable with the distance you have already come. Up there are the real Highlands, but here in Lowland Scotland and the Borders are relaxed, easy-going communities where you can easily be accepted as a local after scarcely more than a decade; most of which you will spend mastering the myriad interpretations of the word 'Imph'm'. Settling into Edinburgh is even easier, and only entails three essentials: remember that the old tower above the east end of Waverley Station is not the Castle but the Calton Gaol; learn to be disrespectful about the Scott Monument (that thing like a baroque

Below:
This view of Waverley's west end from atop the Scott Monument in August 1955 catches some of the steam engines most associated with the district. From bottom to top: a 'Scottish Director', possibly No 62690 *The Lady of the Lake*; 'J83' 0-6-0T No 68473; 'V1' 2-6-2T No 67670; an 'A3' 4-6-2; and a 'B1' 4-6-0.
Mrs A. Hatherill

space-rocket in the Princes Street Gardens); and when the one o'clock gun goes off, do not jump out check your watch. So what are the shocks? Well one is called *Uisge Beatha* (anglice Whisky), another is that everything stops at 10pm.

One of Edinburgh's glories is Waverley, whose location and layout afford, in the writer's view, the finest station in Britain. It lies in a space 1028yds long between Calton Hill and The Mound, an artificial causeway built across the loch which once occupied the area. There has been a station here since 1846, but it was completely rebuilt in the years 1892-97 to cope with the revolution in travel brought about by the building of the Forth Bridge. The only major change since then has been a resignalling in 1936, when the present East and West signalboxes were built. The station is a single vast platform, whose outer sides where through lines pass can each accommodate two full-length trains and are worked as two platforms. Terminal roads are set into each end, and the number is brought up to 21 by an extra platform outside the south side of the overall roof, used mostly for local trains and known as the 'Sub'. The offices are located in the middle, with a grand hall which has a superb mosaic floor with a North British Railway Crest in each corner. The only aspect which jars is that the entire roof seems rather squashed down and even the main buildings are only two storeys high; this results from an Act of

Waverley east end on 8 October 1960. The 'V1' engine is pulling out with the 1.2pm local to Gorebridge on the Waverley route and is signalled to the north running line. The engine whose steam is prominent down by the roof is also signalled out, on the south line. The goods yard and east pilots are diesels. On the right, GPO vans are parked in Calton Road. Beyond the station rise the buildings of the Old Town and distant through the smoke the Castle. *S. Rickard*

Parliament of 1816, granted to the residents of Princes Street, which prohibited the erection of any building on the south side of the street that stood above road level. The only exception is the North British Hotel which stands on the site of an earlier tenement. It has a basement entrance directly off the station. On the other side of the North Bridge (the bridges are omitted from the diagram for simplicity) a siding goes into the basement of the General Post Office; on the south side the national daily paper, The Scotsman, has its own loading dock right outside its door, and several private sidings serve the Fruit Market.

Haymarket station, three miles to the west, was the terminus of the Edinburgh & Glasgow Railway before the line through Princes Street Gardens was built to link it to Waverley. The locomotive depot was part of the 1892 expansion, built on a 'green field' site outside the built-up area, and is thus convenient and spacious if somewhat windswept. It is laid out to allow the routine servicing of engines to be carried out without excessive shunting about and congestion. Arriving engines run either onto or past the turntable and then pass under the overhead coaling plant to refuel, and on to the ash pits where their fires are removed or cleaned. They move into the west end of the shed for examination, servicing and cleaning, and emerge from the east end ready to go off for their next turns of duty. On the north side of the shed is a repair shop, and on the edge of the site a siding for the breakdown crane. Haymarket deals almost entirely with express work, so 70 of the 81 engines based here are passenger types, including seven of the 'A4s'. Local shunting work around Haymarket, Gorgie East and Gorgie Market is covered by two of the little North British tanks of Class J88 and five of the 'J83' 0-6-0Ts which have been the pilots at Waverley for over 50 years.

Goods work is handled by the former North British depot of St Margaret's. The Lothians are not generally regarded as an industrial district in comparison with Clydeside, but in the Edinburgh and Bathgate area on each weekday there are 48 engines available to Control orders for shunting and local freight movements, in addition to those on scheduled trains, to provide for which St Margaret's has an allocation of no fewer than 200 engines ranging from the 'V2' class to the little saddle-tanks called the 'Y9s'. If all those needed shed attention at once there would be chaos, but

most of them spend their time at a multitude of out-stations, collecting goods from such locations as the Lochend Steel Works, Balcarres Street Manure Depot or the sidings of Boglehole and Windygoul.

For our trip on the 'Non-Stop' this day, the engine is from King's Cross: No 60022 *Mallard*. She was built at Doncaster Railway Works to order No EO342, issued in November 1936 for a batch of 10 'A4s', and was completed on 3 March 1938. She was the first of the class to be fitted with a double chimney, which was expected to give an improvement in performance, and consequently was selected for some tests of the Westinghouse Quick Service Application brake valve during which Gresley intended to attempt the rail speed record. On 3 July, hauling a 'Coronation' train set, she attained 126mph

on the down-grade between Little Bytham and Essendine, although in the process her middle big-end ran hot and melted the bearing metal. She went for overhaul after running 80,000 miles in the first year, but when the war came she was put into store. In 1943 she came back into use, but received no special attention until the British Railways test runs of 1948, for which she was refurbished, given the plaques acknowledging the record which she still carries, and paired with one of the corridor tenders. Since then she has been treated as a star. Although she is not a regular on the 'Non-Stop' she does it on occasions, the double-chimney engines being preferred as they have the edge on the others. Her last general overhaul was in February 1954, but she was in works again in November following a minor collision, and is in good condition. The boiler she now carries, No 29315, is much younger than the rest of her; it was built in late 1951 and was first put on no less an engine than *Silver Link*. The tender, No 5648, was new in 1937 and first ran with *Woodcock*.

Besides being the fastest steam engine in the world, *Mallard* is one of the joint holders of the distance record for steam, as on 15 September 1948 she worked the up 'Non-Stop' via Galashiels and Kelso, 408½ miles to London. This was during the period when the main line was devastated by floods, and several crews made the run over the diversion without the booked stops for water or assistance.

Haymarket shed, seven in the morning. A bit early to a Sassenach, maybe, but at this latitude it has been broad daylight for a good three hours. By arriving now, in time to see the daily goods for the Corstorphine branch leave the yard and the 2.0am goods from Stirling arrive behind a 'Caley' engine, we may join *Mallard* on the preparation pit and enjoy the sight, unusual in these days, of an engine being polished. The muckiest part of the cleaning, the wheels and motion, is delegated to the most junior member of the gang of cleaners, a youngster who looks as if still wet behind the ears. Closer inspection shows that this is in fact what he is. It could be that he normally takes his bath by standing under a water column — in Edinburgh in the 1950s there are still plenty of families living in the old miners' rows — or it could be the result of

Left:
On the preparation pit at the east end of Haymarket shed, *Commonwealth of Australia* is ready for duty on 7 August 1960.
Kevin Hughes

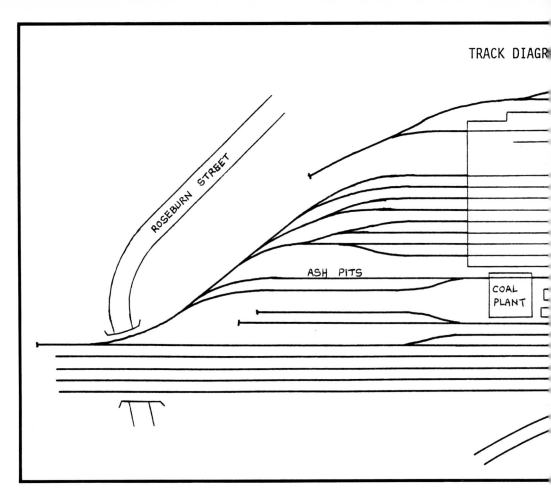

ROSEBURN STREET

ASH PITS

COAL
PLANT

some horseplay which was terminated when the day-shift gaffer arrived. The bosses tolerate these goings-on, not because they want to turn their recruits into hooligans but because they wish those boys to prove to themselves, and to others, that they've got what it takes. In any case, they probably could not curb them, for many conciliation grade staff on the railway come from pretty tough backgrounds. Genteel upbringing and prep-schools may be good enough for those who will never have to do anything more important than scribble figures on bits of paper, but to raise men who can raise steam, run trains and carry in their hands the lives and livelihoods of thousands of people, requires a harder school. Steel and steam make no concessions to anyone's feelings. The youth who can stand the ragging he gets, and stay cheerful, may grow into the man who can be relied on to turn out at two o'clock on a winter morning, get in the pit and fit brake-blocks on an engine, and fit them right. He may acquire the hands and eyes behind which 400 passengers

can relax, knowing that he knows precisely where he is and what to do in any eventuality. He may even become a man who can fire and drive the 'A4' on the 'Elizabethan'.

By eight o'clock the four main line men are signing on and reading the notices. The Haymarket fireman is greeting a friend of his who has just passed as a driver and is taking duty E234, the 'J83' going off at 9.35am to shunt at Gorgie. The examining fitter is giving a clean bill of health to not only *Mallard* but also the engines for the 10.0am, the 10.5am, and the 11.0am and the spare, all now standing outside the east end of the shed. *Mallard* has been examined and oiled, but the drivers inspect her; if anything goes wrong on the road they will be called to account

Right:
The Ransome & Rapier turntable at Haymarket. In this view *Gannet* is backing off it, having turned after working the down 'Non-Stop' on 17 August 1954.
O. M. Richards

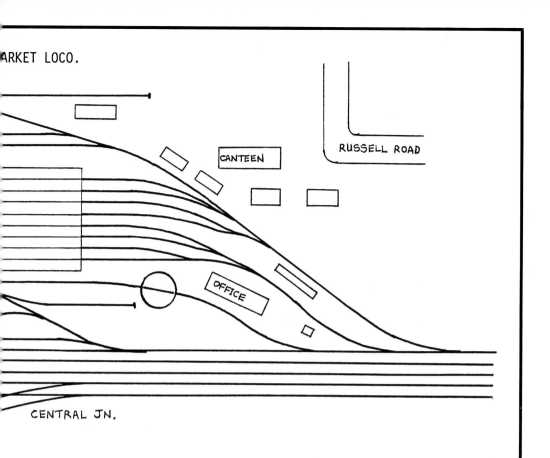

ARKET LOCO.

CANTEEN

RUSSELL ROAD

OFFICE

CENTRAL JN.

for it. (The reader will forgive this sentence for covering a topic which would require a book twice the size of this one.) She is also fully fuelled; the tender has a mountain of coal piled up to the last possible lump. The fireman checks the smokebox door is tight shut before winding the casing hatch, the 'cod's mouth', shut with a crank handle which he takes back to the cab. There is very little fire in the firebox, but this suits him as he can now begin building it up with chosen lumps about 6in across, mostly packed into the back corners of the box. The most important thing, which he checks as soon as he arrives, is the boiler water level, standing about mid-way up the gauge-glass. Steam pressure is only about 150lb, but there is plenty of time yet. About half an hour later it is brought up to 180lb for testing the all-important injectors. The exhaust steam injector cannot be proved when standing still, so the best we can do is test the automatic shuttle valve which switches it from live to exhaust and is controlled by a connection from the engine main steam pipe. After starting the injector on live steam, open the regulator (with of course the brake hard on) and the shuttle valve should operate, and since there is no exhaust steam the injector will knock off, restarting when the regulator is shut.

Above:
An LNER standard coaling plant. This is actually the one at York, seen in June 1965: on the original print the Minster is visible above the 'A1' and 'V2' engines in the background. The coal dropping into the tender of the 'B1' class engine is metered, and recorded against the engine number in the control cabin on the left.
J. R. P. Hunt

Above right:
Your locomotive for today, No 60022 *Mallard*. This view shows her in the final phase of her career, with an AWS receiver under the front end and overhead wire warning labels on the side. The position of the radius rod in the top half of the expansion link shows that she is moving backwards.
E. Oldham

Right:
During the 1948 Locomotive Trials *Mallard* worked one of the 'Atlantic Coast Expresses', and here she is leaving Waterloo. The vehicle behind her is the Dynamometer Car, whose principal function is to measure the engine's power output but also carries a lot of other test equipment. The sartorial styles of the onlookers are a study.
Ian Allan Library

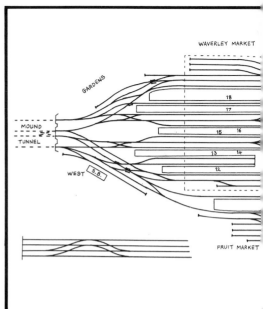

Lastly the headboard. Haymarket can claim to have invented the train headboard, as in 1913 the 'Lothian Coast Express' was the first train to carry its title on the front of the engine. The practice was revived here in 1928 for the 'Flying Scotsman' but was not popular anywhere else until the British Railways era.

At nine o'clock the running foreman appears to check that all is well. The sight of a clean cab, swept floor, vacuum ejector and blower shut off and firedoor closed tells him all he needs to know and the next few minutes find him in the despatcher's tiny hut seeing that all his engines get off shed on time. Sending light engines through to Waverley is a neat embroidery job as they have to be threaded among the service trains. The four main lines are worked as two pairs; the north, 'Fife' up line is occupied in quick succession by the 6.54am from Dundee and the 9.6am from Corstorphine, so before they arrive we are sent across to the south, 'Glasgow' up line. The 'Scotsman' and 'Waverley' engines will follow, coupled together, on the north line.

From Haymarket station the approaching engine appears as a white cloud, moving very slowly and occasionally clearing to reveal the 'A4' nose, as she eases over a crossover to gain the main line and drifts along with no sound other than the throaty roar of steam from the open cylinder drain cocks. Passing under the Caley bridge, she accelerates very gradually through the platforms. It is a cliché to compare a locomotive with a thoroughbred horse, but little else can compare with the majestic slowness, the easy stride of the connecting rod, the wreaths of condensed breath, the quiver of pent-up power. If this thing had been created by an artist he would be hailed as the greatest genius of the 20th century, and every piece of his work would be revered by posterity. Symbolically, *Mallard* vanishes into the darkness of Haymarket tunnel.

Edinburgh Castle, the biggest of several fortresses we will see today and the only one still in use as a military headquarters, towers so close above us as to be invisible from the footplate as we amble through the gardens, using the whistle to greet children on footbridges. Entering Waverley station, we are turned into the right-hand side to run slowly along the through road and stop beside the wall. Here we can exchange pleasantries with the crew of the morning goods yard shunt, make a final check of our fire, and observe the activity around us. Waverley still retains something of the old tradition of trains from all parts bringing businessmen into the city for mid-morning meetings, and at this time is quite lively:

Arrivals
7.20am from Thornton Junction arrives 8.41am
8.33am from Duddingston arrives 8.54am

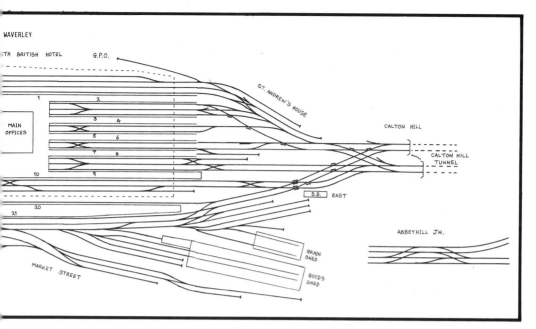

WAVERLEY

NORTH BRITISH HOTEL   G.P.O.

ST. ANDREW'S HOUSE

CALTON HILL

MAIN OFFICES

CALTON HILL TUNNEL

1   2
3   4
5   6
7   8
10   9

S.B. EAST

ABBEYHILL JN.

20
21

MARKET STREET

GRAIN SHED

GOODS SHED

.13am from Berwick arrives 9.6am
.54am from Dundee arrives 9.9am
.48am from Rosewell arrives 9.10am
2.55am from King's Cross arrives 9.17am
.6am from Corstorphine arrives 9.18am
.47am from Aberdeen arrives 9.29am
.10am light engine from Niddrie arrives 9.30am
  (goods yard)
.37am from Hyndland (via Bathgate) arrives
  9.35am
.18am from Musselburgh arrives 9.35am
.7am from Hawick arrives 9.40am
.5am from Stirling arrives 9.42am

Departures
.45am to Perth
.46am to Dunbar
.5am to Glasgow
.10am to Dundee
.45am to King's Cross
0.0am to King's Cross
0.5am to St Pancras

The reader is invited to sit down with the station plan and work out how to fit in that little lot, not forgetting the empty stock and engine movements. Then you can add the goods trains, which are sent round the 'Sub', such as the .15am from Bathgate which passes Haymarket West Junction at 8.23am and reaches Portobello at 9.55am, or the 7.2am from Cadder (Glasgow) to Meadows Yard which follows it half an hour later. And there may be extras; for example on 0 June the Household Cavalry travelled in a special train direct from Kensington Olympia to Gorgie Market Cattle Siding!

The 'Elizabethan' set is brought in from Craigentinny carriage depot and placed in the down platform, No 10, because the 10am 'Flying

Below:
That stalwart of the 'Non-Stop', *Union of South Africa*, had her own emblem, a winged springbok. This shows the version applied by her present owner, Mr John Cameron. At the top left, between the tender side and the flexible canopy, is the roof of the corridor.
J. B. Cameron

60009

33

Above:
Engines running light from Haymarket shed to Waverley: No 60152 *Holyrood* and No 60534 *Irish Elegance* on the up Fife line, in Princes Street Gardens. They are to take on north- and southbound trains respectively. Beside them can be seen a telephone box, a colour-light signal for the down Fife line and on the up Glasgow line a treadle for registering the presence of a train. In the background is the Caledonian Hotel — the rival firm.
R. Leslie

Scotsman' is loading in Platform No 1 and the 10.5am 'Waverley' is in Platform No 9. The spectacle of these three trains preparing to leave the country is one of the truly great sights of the city whose sons have done so much to spread civilisation across the world. Our train is not complete; we await two through coaches from Aberdeen which form part of the 5.47am. A first task on arrival is to ascertain from Control how that train is running, as arrivals from the north are being affected by Civil Engineers' work on Jamestown Viaduct, between North Queensferry and Inverkeithing, which is causing delays and complete closure of the line on Sundays. It is reported three minutes late. As soon as the stock is in position we get the signal to draw forward and back on. A group of spectators watches us approach them at a slow walk, the guard beckoning and a shunter standing by with his eye on the buckeye coupling standing open on the leading coach. The 'A4' tenders were fitted with buckeyes from new, which shows that it is not a new idea — it was introduced by the Great Northern Railway in 1898. The engine has to be driven gently against the train to make the coupling snap shut, and there is a jerk as she is held captive. To make sure, the shunter calls 'Ease

Away' and we put her in forward gear and open the regulator momentarily; then since we stay put, he goes beneath to connect up the vacuum pipe. The roar of steam from the cocks dies away and *Mallard* stands quiet, just a drift of smoke rising to the roof girders. The King's Cross fireman, who got off as soon as we arrived, reappears to put on the engine a vital item – the tea – then the London men retire to the train where the first compartment is reserved for them. All this is watched by a smart gentleman standing nearby, Mr Arnott the stationmaster, who has stepped out to check his organisation's performance at the highlight of its day. For our part, we are ready to go.

In Full Flight

At 9.30am the Aberdeen train draws up in Waverley's Platform No 11. At 9.33am its engine is running forward over the central crossover and the west end pilot is buffering up at the rear. At 9.35am the through coaches are pushed up to the rear of the 'Elizabethan'. At 9.38am a rasping roar comes from the front end as the driver turns on his vacuum ejector for a brake test. At 9.40am the station announcer's clear Scottish lilt is requesting passengers to join the train and a platform inspector is closing the brake van doors on the small consignment of parcels and mail privileged to travel with us. It is now 9.44am and the starter signal goes to green. The brake ejector goes on again to release the brakes. 9.45am: the guard's shrill whistle is answered by the chime whistle, the driver winds his reverser to full forward and opens the regulator slightly.

All other sounds are drowned in the blast of steam from the cylinder cocks as steam-chest pressure climbs to near 100lb, then *Mallard* begins to inch forward. Approaching the platform end the fireman shuts the cocks and in the sudden quiet the heavy beat from the chimney becomes audible, still pacing out a slow measure. The south bore of Calton Hill Tunnel swallows us. In the darkness the exhaust noise dies away as the engine is brought up to 25% cut-off. This is the steepest gradient on the entire route, a descent at 1 in 78 which rolls us out of the city without effort, past the bulk of Arthur's Seat on our right and the Abbeyhill curve on our left. Wheels begin to hum on rails and our engine takes up the sway and swing of motion which will be unceasing for the next six and a half hours. The driver reaches out and holds the whistle open as we approach St Margaret's and notice what a cramped site it is. The engine shed lies on the south side of the line but has its main offices in the old works on the other side, connected by a foot crossing which is out of sight

Above left:
'J83' No 68481 as Waverley west end pilot, prepares to remove a train from No 15 Platform at 12.5pm on 31 August 1956. The engine is a credit to the men of Haymarket. The nearest doors on the coach show a feature of the BR carmine and cream ('blood and custard') livery: grey panels on the double doors for chalking up destinations.
G. W. Morrison

Left:
A view across the east end of Waverley showing St Andrew's House, the Scottish government office, built on the site of Calton Gaol. The engine is *Flying Scotsman*, backing into Platform No 10 to work the very last 'Non-Stop' on 4 May 1968.
SHA

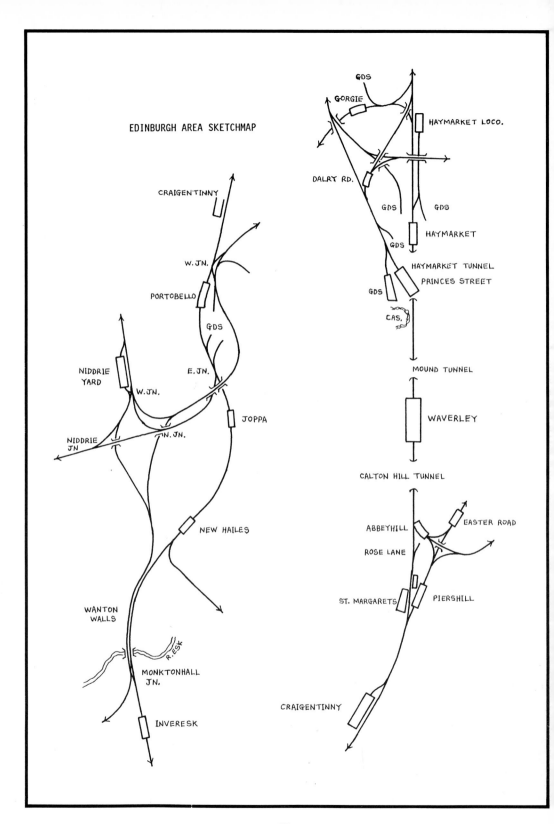

EDINBURGH AREA SKETCHMAP

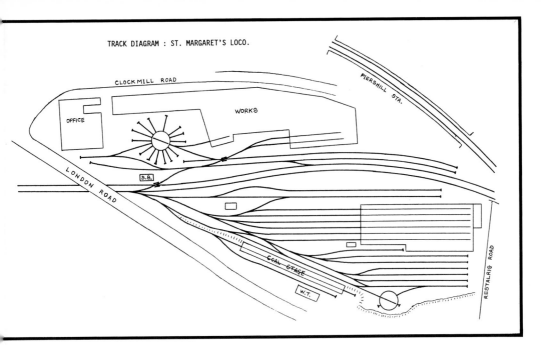

TRACK DIAGRAM : ST. MARGARET'S LOCO.

Below:
St Margarets shed had to provide a Class 5 engine to stand by in Waverley station. On 7 May 1966, near the end of steam, it is No 45483. Beyond, 2-6-4T No 80114 is taking an empty train out. The north and south bores of Calton Hill Tunnel lie in the left background. The blank foreground is the site of the engine spurs off the end of Platforms Nos 7/8.
SHA

until we come through the bridge a few yards from it, and is further obscured by an engine standing near the bridge. This is a 'B1' 4-6-0 waiting to leave the depot and follow us down to Portobello.

All this time our fireman has been sitting relaxed in his seat, unconcerned that pressure is still below 200lb. Past St Margaret's, speed is up to about 40mph and the driver condescends to

open the regulator a little more, but there is still little demand for steam, for within a minute we are coasting again through Portobello station, on a long curve past the platform and the extensive yards. Here is the centre of local freight operation, where there are four shunting engines on duty and four more, chunky North British 0-6-0s, under Control orders for trip workings (a trip is a movement made primarily to suit the convenience of the railway). Ahead, over Portobello East Junction, start of the Waverley route, a goods is crossing on a single-line flyover. It is the

train from Bathgate we mentioned earlier, using the Lothian Lines — a group of freight-only connections built as late as 1913 to connect the coalfield branches with the Port of Leith, Portobello, Meadows Yard and Niddrie Yard. At Newhailes Junction we see above us to the right another freight, headed by the LMS 2-6-0 No 46462 which is kept for working the Gifford and Macmerry branches, making for Monktonhall on the eastern arm of the Lothian Lines, while beyond Monktonhall Junction a freight from England, the 4.45am from Heaton, is waiting at signals for admission to that same route. Further out, at Prestonpans is a 'J38' 0-6-0 with empty wagons he has just lifted from Wallyford Brickworks siding, while in Longniddry yard another 0-6-0 is waiting to join the main line with a goods

from Haddington. In the midst of all this activity the passage of an express seems no more than an interlude, with real work to resume as soon as we are out of the way.

Clear of Portobello, the fire is now livened up and pressure has come round to 230lb, so it is time to get the exhaust injector going. Under the right-hand seat is a water control handle which is set on full. The steam valve on the boiler back-head is turned on slightly, which admits live steam to the injector and opens an automatic water valve so that it starts. The shuttle valve should then open so that it utilises exhaust

Above left:
St Margarets shed yard on 2 March 1966, with four engines alongside the coal stage on the left and 2-6-4Ts Nos 42691 and 80006 parked after disposal. In front of them are stacks of firebricks (for arches) and brake blocks. Ash wagons are standing on a sunken siding.
SHA

Left:
View eastwards at Craigentinny on 2 March 1966. 'V2' No 60836, the last of the class in service, moving out of the carriage sidings with an empty stock working.
SHA

Above:
At Craigentinny box on 4 May 1968, *Flying Scotsman* on the last 'Non-Stop' on her way out of Edinburgh and into history. At that time the northerly pair of tracks from here to Monktonhall were intact but disused.
SHA

steam fed back from the smokebox. Once it is working the steam valve is turned on full and the fireman adjusts the water control to feed as much water to the boiler as is being taken from it. Now he steps down into the middle of the cab. The basic rule when firing the 'A4s' is 'Keep It Thin'. This means he will be shovelling at frequent intervals from here on, a round of eight shovelfuls every minute or so, sometimes more, but with a hard steam coal there is little opportunity to pile a mass in and leave it for any length of time. He must work in close co-ordination with the driver's requirements and not let the engine get out of his control at any moment. The firebox has a hinged door, but that is not opened in normal service, all firing being done through the horizontally pivoted flap. You push it in with the shovel and a ratchet arm drops over the top to hold it open, then afterwards you knock the arm up and it swings shut. With a thin, hot fire, the first coal to go in instantly fills the box with a

Left:
At the west end of Portobello yard, No 65909, a 'J38', a very strong 0-6-0 type peculiar to this area, pulling out past Leith South Junction box with a tank train. The main lines are in the foreground, distinguished by their heavier flat-bottom rails.
J. C. Baker

Bottom left:
What the writer believes to have been the last regular steam operation on the tracks of the East Coast route was here, in the remnants of Niddrie West Yard, where once the international goods trains terminated. The National Coal Board used it for coal from Newcraighall Colliery. Barclay 'pug' No 2358 is seen shunting on 8 June 1967.
SHA

mass of flame, giving plenty of heat on the superheater elements, just what we want because at last, heading out past Wanton Walls, his mate gives her the works. The throttle goes wide open and *Mallard* takes wing.

On this length we are actually heading about East-North-East, parallel to the coast. The distant hills on our left are in the Kingdom of Fife, 15 miles away across the Firth of Forth, and it is said you can walk across through the coal workings from Preston Grange to Seafield on the far side. About half a mile past Prestonpans station the main line crosses the route of the Newbattle-Cockenzie wagonway, at the place where the latter formed the battle line when the Government forces of Sir John Cope were routed by the Jacobites of Charles Edward Stuart in 1745. Between Longniddry and Aberlady Junction, look out on the left for a castle very different in style from Edinburgh: Redhouse Castle, a 16th century tower house. And as a reminder of a more recent conflict, away on the right is a glimpse of the hangars of East Fortune airfield, where No 602 Squadron, together with No 603 from Turnhouse, claimed the first German raiders to be brought down in October 1939. Remote it all seems from today's peaceful scene of some of the finest farmland in the country, bright in the keen, clear air. The coastline goes away northwards to where the Berwick Law shows like a pyramid on the horizon, then as we round the bend through East Linton (birthplace of the engineer John Rennie) the sea is again visible, with another distinctive shape, the Bass Rock, standing out clearly six miles away.

The only trains we shall see on the road from here to Newcastle are, with two exceptions, goods trains; here just for the record is the list:

5.55am Heaton-Niddrie	passes	at East Linton
6.25am Heaton-Meadows		at Dunbar
7.20am Heaton-Granton		at Reston Junction
7.30am Heaton-Niddrie	in the down loop	at Berwick
7.50am Heaton-Tweedmouth	passes	near Scremerston
10pm Thames Wharf-Niddrie		at Crag Mill Siding, near Belford
9.55am Heaton-Niddrie		at Chathill
8.14am York-Edinburgh parcels		at Little Mill

8.55am Heaton-Alnmouth, which should be there by the time we pass
The Amble branch goods, which is clearly late as we find it still shunting at Chevington.

2.30am King's Cross-Niddrie		at Killingworth

43

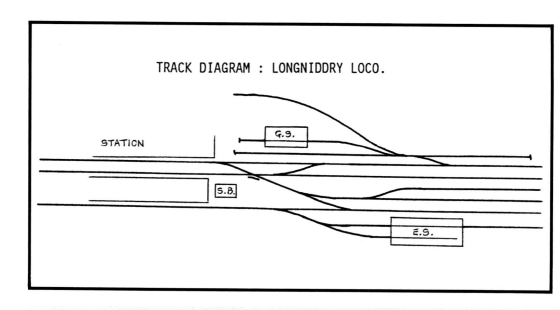

TRACK DIAGRAM : LONGNIDDRY LOCO.

STATION

G.9.

S.B.

E.S.

The passenger trains are the 6.40am York-Edinburgh, which we should pass near Beal, and the 9.15am Leeds-Glasgow, near Cramlington. In addition, while we are cruising along the cliff by Hilton Bay we pass a heavy train consisting entirely of pigeon vans. The birds are not, I hasten to add, for eating; they are racing pigeons on their way to the north to be released, a well-organised routine which brings a lot of business to the railways. And in the yard at Dunbar is a real gem: a North British 'Glen'. Her job is to

spend the day pottering about between East Linton and Grantshouse on what is known as the 'Dunbar Shunt'.

Now how is *Mallard* doing? As she warms up she is accelerating gently but continuously until on the long descent past Drem she is up to 80mph even though we start easing the regulator back. Allow the speed to fall away to 60mph by East Fortune, and let her run with the reverser up to near the 15% mark and 80-100lb in the steam chest, at which she speeds up again to 70mph. As the spire of Dunbar church comes in sight the driver shuts the regulator altogether, noting with a corner of his mind that the injector is picking up on live steam as it should, and lets her coast at 60mph round the curve on the through line outside the station. The pressure gauge is on the 250lb mark and the fireman has built his fire up appreciably thicker than it was when we started, but now he leaves it alone while she blasts away up the 1 in 200 gradient out of Dunbar, really working for her living now.

On the level again, he does some fast stoking, and note that this time besides firing to the back and sides he is directing coal to different parts of the grate, with several pauses to peer under the inverted shovel blade at the inferno. Not that these engines are tricky for steam, but care is needed to get the most out of them and keep the pressure up to the mark when faced with full regulator and 25%.

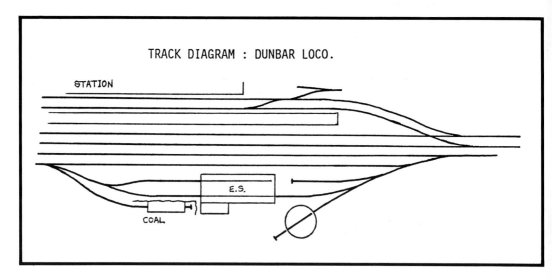

TRACK DIAGRAM : DUNBAR LOCO.

STATION

E.S.

COAL

Our driver is clearly a man who believes in giving everyone a comfortable ride on the bends and using the whip on the straights, for as speed rises again to 80mph he sits back in an attitude of leisure to enjoy the sight of his mate working up a sweat, and when the latter looks round at the cut-off scale he merely grins. South of the Dunglass viaduct, past the little village of Cockburnspath (pronounced Co-path) is the severest incline on the line, 4½ miles at 1 in 96. *Mallard* flings herself up it with a glorious enthusiasm; above the booming echo of the blast in the fire-box we hear her voice in a harsh rippling roar from the chimney and the fire is a pure white, raking our legs with its radiant claws when the flap is opened. Ahead the mass of Penmanshiel Moor blocks our way until railway and road turn into the defile of the Pease Burn, up which lorries

Left:
On Saturday 27 July 1955 an engine was required to work a special down from Newcastle on the Bank Holiday Monday. St Margarets sent 'B1' No 61191, attached to the 10.10am up and coupled, according to standard practice, behind the train engine *Golden Plover*. Seen on Cockburnspath Bank. In the normal way double-heading was unusual on the East Coast route.
C. J. B. Sanderson

Above:
The 11am Edinburgh-King's Cross at speed going up Cockburnspath Bank: locomotive *Empire of India*. On the right are a 1 in 96 gradient post and Milepost 39, by Broad Wood where the road nears the railway.
H. K. Harman

can be seen grinding, each with its tail of frustrated speedsters. Our speed comes down, 60mph, 50mph. The fireman shuts the flap and cuts the feed back to minimum for the climb, taking his seat as she hammers through the 267yd Penmanshiel Tunnel. Now down to 45mph, which is about right for the curves over the top and past the isolated station of Grantshouse, in a remarkably mountainous set-

ting although it is only 400ft above sea level. As she turns the summit the boiler water level drops to near the bottom of the glass, but this is deliberate so that when the driver almost shuts the regulator and winds the reverser back to near mid-gear, the injector can go on full to hold pressure at 230lb. It is even possible to come over to the driver's side and start up the left-hand, live steam, injector and then take our time about replenishing the fire while the train gathers speed down the hill. The driver consults his watch. It is just half-past ten, and he is so pleased with the response of the engine that he rewards his mate with a paean of praise: 'Aye, imph'm'.

On the way down there are seven bridges over the Eye Water, all modern structures, and thereby hangs a tale — of 11 and 12 August 1948, when a terrific storm broke over the Borders and lashed them with wind and rain. Little burns became giants, tossing the works of Man aside with a fine contempt; the line from Reston Junction to St Boswells was wrecked and never reopened, while the Eye Water took out the seven bridges and a viaduct on the Eyemouth branch, and Penmanshiel Tunnel was turned into an aqueduct. (The tragedy of this event matured in its own good time, for in 1979 when work began to enlarge the bore of the tunnel for electric trains, the roof collapsed, killing two men,

Above left:
The 'Talisman', the 4pm Edinburgh-King's Cross, coming out of Penmanshiel Tunnel and under the Great North Road on 22 June 1959. Immediately in front of the engine, *William Whitelaw*, the permanent way changes from bull-head to flat-bottom rails, necessitating special fishplates at the joins. This is the piece of line that was abandoned after the catastrophic collapse of the tunnel.
H. K. Harman

Left:
Coming up to the summit at Blackburnrig, *Sir Murrough Wilson*, cleaned on the front and nowhere else, on 26 June 1954. The first vehicle is one of a small number of bogie brake vans built with only two sets of doors, followed by a Gresley brake/third.
E. D. Bruton

Top:
A close-up of the down side border sign. It is 9ft high and 14ft across, and bears on the left a Rose, St George's Cross and a Lion Rampant, and on the right a Thistle, St Andrew's Cross and a Unicorn. Below is the boundary post between York and Edinburgh mileages.
I. S. Carr

and eventually the tunnel was abandoned and by-passed.) Not the first time the weather has taken control, for in 1881 a storm took 129 souls from the fishing port of Eyemouth. A beautiful country, yes, but a hard one, where even in high summer, as we run along the cliffs a biting wind comes in the cab side to remind us that there is nothing between this coast and the North Pole.

Remember to turn off the live steam injector before the boiler gets too full. If the exhaust injector is a good one it can be cut right down to continue matching its delivery to consumption. When not firing the fireman stays in his seat, partly to watch the road and partly to keep away from the heat. A hinged steel barrier plate is attached on each side of the firehole, and with a good fire of hard coal they are a real comfort.

Swinging easily into the fast curves, *Mallard* cruises on at 60-65mph, held in check for the corner at Ayton. Across the valley the noble pile is Ayton Castle, not a real castle but a residence in the style called 'Scottish Baronial', completed in 1843. Through Burnmouth, and here we are on a wonderful cliff-top run with a vast open sea view alternating with sheltered cutting sides where primroses flower. At 70mph the English border is crossed just north of Marshall Mead-

ows Bay. The Great North Road crossing is nearby, at Lamberton Toll House, the eastern equivalent to the Gretna smithy but for some reason far less famous. At this spot the line as built was found to be rather too close to the edge of the cliffs for comfort, so it was moved in 1885 and the old course is visible on our left. At the far end of the deviation is Marshall Meadows signalbox, which is important as it marks the boundary between the Scottish and North Eastern Regions. This is the point where it is diplomatically sound to be on time, so we are glad to note that we are entering England two minutes ahead of schedule, and that will go on record. The driver actually shuts off steam completely here, and eases the brake handle down a little until the train-pipe vacuum gauge needle falls from 21 to 15in of vacuum and the brakes come

Previous page:
On 24 October 1948, one of the temporary replacements for the seven bridges over the Eye Water; this is No 133. The structure is under a load test, with *Commonwealth of Australia* and 'Shire' 4-4-0 *Forfarshire* providing the load. It is hard to imagine the trickle of water in the bottom there taking out a whole bridge.
British Railways

on gently to bring us down to the 30mph limit through Berwick. The first 57 miles have taken 58 min, and a mix of skill, experience and teamwork made it look quite easy.

Exchanging greetings with the crew of the 'V2' on the down goods train, we run under the main road into Berwick-upon-Tweed station, which is built on the site of the castle — a piece of wall is still standing behind the goods yard but is obscured by a train on the down side of the single platform. It is customary to accuse Robert Stephenson of an act of vandalism in putting his railway slap through a mediaeval banqueting hall, but the fact is of course that the locals had not regarded the castle as anything more than a source of building stone for ages, and the station, built in 1927, is a handsome asset to this ancient town. Off the platform end we are straight onto the Royal Border Bridge, named as such by Queen Victoria although it is not strictly on the border. Perhaps she, like many of us, felt that Berwick is spiritually in Scotland despite being ceded to England in 1485 after changing sides 14 times. After crossing it the line turns through a right angle and by looking back you will see it, 28 arches totalling 720yd, carrying the rails 126ft above the river bed, built by Mackay and Blackstock of Cumberland for £263,000. Equally advanced in its way is the Old Bridge.

When King James VI passed through on his way to take over the English throne, he remarked that he did not think much of the bridge; the town took the hint and a new one was completed in 1643 and carried all road traffic until the Royal Tweed Bridge was built in 1928.

Under easy steam we cross the bridge, well inside the 50mph limit, to Tweedmouth with its yard and engine shed. The route used by the 1948 record runs comes in from the right here, and the train we saw in Berwick station had come over it — the 8.33am from St Boswells. We are beside the sea again for a short distance until the line has descended to sea level and the water is obscured by sand hills. The dip through Beal would be a fine racing stretch were it not for the speed limit of 80mph, which is held comfortably on the level past Lindisfarne. Prominent on the right-hand end of the island is another castle, but this one is a fake, as it was rebuilt in 1903. Belford station is marked by a large rock outcrop on the up side, and shortly afterwards the fireman steps over to the driver's side and takes a chain off the water scoop handle. The up-grade has slowed the train and at Lucker station the engine is eased to bring speed down to about 60mph in the next mile. As soon as we are over Lucker water trough he winds the scoop down as fast as he can and waits until his mate, watching ahead, makes a chopping gesture in what is obviously an accustomed routine, when he winds it up equally smartly having collected as much water as possible in the 600yd length of the trough. The device for checking the tender water level is remarkably crude, comprising a large upright pipe which you rotate by pulling a handle. When turned it reveals a series of small holes, corresponding to thousand-gallon levels, and you tell where the water is by which holes it issues from. This was found to be inadequate for determining when the tank is full in the few seconds over a water trough, so an overflow pipe is provided, emerging on the tender front and discharging into a funnel and drain-pipe. When water starts pouring from this pipe the scoop must be raised at once or the tank filler at the back will do its impression of a fountain.

It looks as though it was a good pick-up, as the tank is nearly full again, and we are set for the climb to Little Mill.

Left:
The Royal Border Bridge, with *Sir Nigel Gresley* heading south on her Doncaster-Edinburgh tour of 20 August 1967. In former times the signal was a gantry astride the bridge. Berwick station is off to the left, and the masonry in the foreground is part of the castle.
C. F. Burton

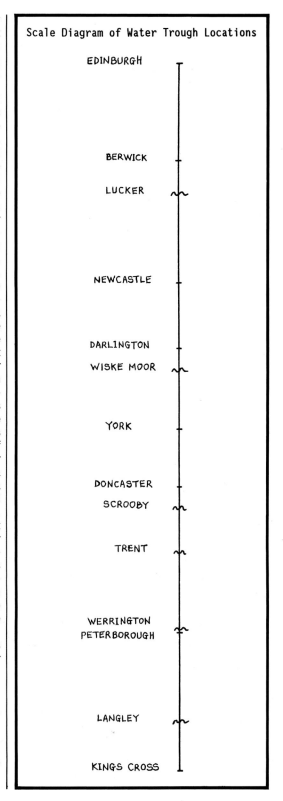

Scale Diagram of Water Trough Locations

EDINBURGH

BERWICK

LUCKER

NEWCASTLE

DARLINGTON

WISKE MOOR

YORK

DONCASTER

SCROOBY

TRENT

WERRINGTON

PETERBOROUGH

LANGLEY

KINGS CROSS

Through Northumberland and Durham

Mallard romps up the 1 in 150 gradient from Chathill to Stamford Crossing with little extra effort, full regulator taking her over the top at a little over 60mph. The fireman does not fire on the bank, leaving the flap shut so as to avoid admitting cold air above the fire. With no fresh coal emitting volatile matter the air supply is wanted coming up through the grate to keep the body of fire at maximum temperature, so that there is not only ample steam but also effective superheating, meaning that what steam is used is good and hot. He even shuts the injector right off and again allows the water to come right down. Once over the top the fire will still be hot, but we cannot let her rip downhill because there is a 60mph limit at the bottom through Alnmouth, so he uses the excess heat to fill the boiler instead; thus evening out the workload, which is good for both him and his boiler. You will also have noticed by now that he times his firing to be

in his seat looking ahead on the approach to each signalbox, station and level crossing. He never sits down for long, however, as even while she is careering down the bank he is putting in the fire that will be needed in a few minutes' time. The brake is on to steady her over the Aln viaduct, past the Alnwick branch curving in on the right. Alnmouth station is just the sort that would make a good model, with a branch line, bay platform, a small engine shed, and goods yard with a typical set of North Eastern coal drops (a siding on trestles at which carts can be

Below:
This elegant country house is Beal station, an important alighting point for tourists bound for Holy Island. When this photograph was taken in July 1977 it was used as a private house and the platforms had been demolished.
SHA

loaded straight from wagons). The town of Aln-mouth lies on a headland on the far side of the River Aln estuary and is presented in a splendid vista from the line south of the station. This is also our last view of the sea.

Now a new theme enters the view from the footplate: coal. South Shilbottle is the first colliery, a reminder that we are heading for the heart of the Tyne coalfield. As yet it is only an intrusion, for as we push on past Warkworth station and over a viaduct across the wooded valley of the Coquet, we see Acklington and Widdrington with their brickworks. The big airfield at Acklington is associated with the most successful air action of 1940, as it was the base of No 72 Squadron who on the 15 August engaged and repulsed a raiding force that outnumbered them 10 to 1.

The view through the front window is changing to spoil tips and smoking chimneys. Ten minutes at a steady 70mph bring us to Pegswood and a long viaduct over the River Wansbeck, which is the point to shut off for Morpeth's 40mph limit. The fireman does a little sorting out in his department, taking advantage of the lack of strong draught to examine the fire and lift one or two dead spots with the straight poker. He drives his shovel up into the front of the coal

Above:

The view of Newcastle from the Castle. The famous crossings are on the left where tracks diverge onto the High Level Bridge. The foreground trackwork is complicated by electro-pneumatic point machines and odd lengths of rail which are power rails for the electric trains. Note the garden in front of the hut on the right. Below, Westgate Road is laid with tram tracks, and the building with three gables is labelled 'LNER Parcels Dept'. This view was taken on 28 July 1948 and shows *Commonwealth of Australia* **in BR blue livery, the Thompson coaches being in imitation teak colour. The train, the down 'Flying Scotsman', is coming through Central station under No 1 signalbox; the up train would use the track immediately to its left.**
K. C. Footer

heap in the tender, which causes some dust and small coal to come down. This he stows into the box, flicking the shovel so that it sprays over the hot fire and burns up instantly, the blower being on and the flap door left open to clear the resultant smoke before we run through Morpeth.

Although Morpeth is a country town, its station forms a junction with the northern end of the Blyth & Tyne system, serving the coalfield, and with that heroic, if quite uncommercial, line of

55

the North British which wanders over the hills to Reedsmouth. On either side of the main line appear the pithead towers and pit villages: Dinnington, Seghill, Seaton Delaval — names redolent of dark galleries, fire-damp and slow clanking trains from mine to staith and back again. As we go south the biting wind is replaced by the sulphurous miasma of industry — the pollution which measures human prosperity. However, there is still plenty of countryside around, such as the rural corridor of the River Blyth seen from the viaduct near Plessey Hall.

Our driver gives *Mallard* the gun again and is soon cracking along at 70mph, but at Cramlington we get the distant signal 'on'. So far we have had the railway pretty much to ourselves, allowing our timekeeping to fluctuate but usually keeping comfortably a few minutes ahead of schedule; the men of Haymarket are in the habit of declaiming how much lost time they retrieve between Newcastle and Edinburgh, but the fact is that they may have the road to contend with, but nothing like the traffic that has to be knitted together south of the Tyne. The reader unfamiliar with railway operation might have seen those arena displays where Army motor-cycle riders go weaving between one another from all directions. If you imagine a similar game being played over miles of country, with units moving at various speeds and subject to a host of gremlins, traceable only by a network of telephones, you may gain some idea of what the Newcastle Control are dealing with. At 11.42am a goods train from Normanton is due through Newcastle and along the North Shields line to arrive in Heaton south yard by 11.55am. At 11.45am an electric train is due to start from Central station, running down the main line as far as Manors where it turns off northwards. At the same time another one comes in over the High Level Bridge from South Shields and crosses over the main lines to reach the terminal platforms. And, a steam train goes off and turns right over the bridge for Sunderland. At 11.51am the 'Non-Stop' passes. At 11.53am a train comes in from Sunderland. While this is happening at the east end of the station, the west end also has an 11.45am departure to Hexham on the Carlisle line and an 11.53am arrival from Blackhill via Ouston Junction, but these movements can take place without conflicting. Until recently it was busier still, for services from Blackhill via the Derwent Valley and Beamish only ceased in May 1955.

Newcastle's first passenger station was the Newcastle & Carlisle terminus at Redheugh, almost underneath where the King Edward

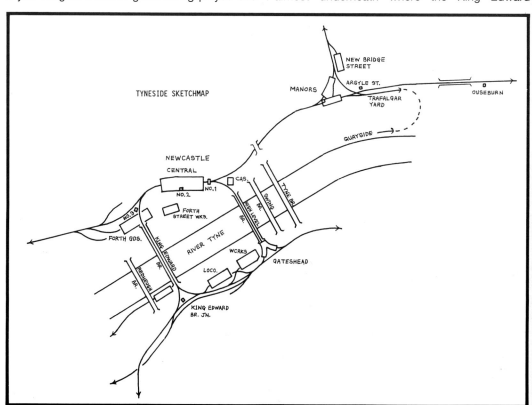

TYNESIDE SKETCHMAP

Bridge is now, where a few overgrown sidings run along the uninviting riverside. Central station was opened by Queen Victoria on a whistle-stop journey on 29 August 1850, when she also dedicated the Royal Border Bridge. It was later enlarged at the east end, with the result that crammed in between the platform ends and the Castle keep is a formation of 21 track crossings, incorporating 84 crossing assemblies, which instead of being built-up from rail are castings in high-grade tool steel, bolted up into one gigantic unit the better to withstand the intensive use they receive. Nine tracks are provided across the broad barrier of the Tyne, three on the High Level Bridge, four on the King Edward Bridge and with

Below:
A view of the King Edward Bridge taken from a northbound train, looking towards Newcastle with St John's church spire in the distance. The long building on the far side is Forth goods station, with the main line sliced through it near the right-hand end. Four of the LNER metal signs were mounted on the bridge and are just visible in front of the engine. The train is *Sir Nigel Gresley's* Peterborough-Newcastle tour on 23 July 1967.
SHA

a short diversion up river, two on Scotswood Bridge, and the circular layout allows a unique flexibility in operation. A train approaching on any route can pass through Central in either direction and can double back on its tracks without having to reverse. On the south bank of the river is the Gateshead works and running shed complex, where some heavy repair work is still carried on although the works were closed in 1932 and reopened to meet the wartime demands for engineering capability which the railways did so much to fill. Close by Central station is another famous locomotive building centre, the Forth Street Works established by the Stephensons, birthplace of the most celebrated locomotive of all — *Rocket.*

This day the passing time of the 'Non-Stop' at Morpeth is telephoned to Control, so they know where we are, but the down goods train is late, so the controller orders it to be placed in one of the loops which pass outside Central station. The 'Non-Stop' will now have to go through platform No 9, so No 2 signalbox is instructed to clear it, and since the local movements are all slightly late the signalmen at Cramlington, Dam Dykes, Dudley and Killingworth are told to put their distant signals against the train and slow it down. When the driver comes into sight of the

Above:
It would be a great mistake to think of County Durham as all pit-banks. This is another view of *SNG* on 23 July 1967, crossing Plawsworth Viaduct heading south.
D. E. Gouldthorpe

Cramlington home, with his brake well on ready to stop at it, and sees it and the starter signal moving to 'clear' in front of him he knows what is going on, and applies just a breath of steam to keep *Mallard* jogging along at about 50mph. The fireman packs up firing altogether and closes down the ashpan damper. In this manner, at the end of the second hour, we come down past Dudley Colliery, where a Coal Board tank engine is at work among masses of wagons, under a line which serves the Burradon, Weetslade, Shankhouse, Hazelrigg, Havannah and Seaton Burn collieries, and through Killingworth station (actually in West Moor). South of the station a road passes below, and a few hundred yards along to our left lies George Stephenson's house.

The Stephensons moved into the Killingworth cottage in 1804, just after Robert's birth, when George became Brakesman at West Moor Col-

liery, and lived there for 20 years until they began travelling world-wide. As we are on a railway engine it is natural that we should think first of the development of the locomotive as their great achievement of that period, although locally George is revered more for his invention of the miners' safety lamp. But what made him a great man was that he was a true egalitarian, equally at home dining in princes' palaces or in labourers' back houses and treating all men alike. Sadly the fruits of engineering have since often been used not to liberate the working man but to line the pockets of the privileged, yet the steam engine has retained its quality of cutting across class and status to bring people together in a common affection, a feature that should secure its permanent place in the world even after it has been discarded as a tool for pure commerce. If the authorities wish to reconcile the divisions in 20th century society they should note this, and take action.

Into the spread of sidings at Heaton, into an uncompromising mass of heavy industry, through the passenger station, a gloomy place brightened only by nameboards in a bright orange which is the house colour of the North Eastern Region, at an easy 30mph. We keep the engine from blowing off by use of the live-steam injector, partly to avoid spilling water on the electric third-rail which is installed on the main line as far as Benton Quarry Junction. Byker station appears on our left on a sharply curved branch that goes immediately into a tunnel, then we roll across the Ouseburn Viaduct and slower still the train snakes through Manors station. Against the retaining wall on the left you will see a still-working NER signal, whose arm works in a slot in the post. Ahead the smoke-blackened castle keep looks not so very distinct from the massive warehouses, symbols of the modern ruling factions. We have a clear road! At 15mph we enter the huge overall roof, bustling platforms whose denizens stop to regard us as a world apart, their conversations interrupted by a shrieking of wheel flanges and the chatter of *Mallard's* exhaust as the driver gives her more steam. The time is 11.54am, so we are three minutes late. In one of the west end bay platforms is the Hexham train, late leaving, with a 'G5' 0-4-4T blowing off impatiently, and the Blackwell train runs in hauled by one of the last of the 'N8' class, an 0-6-2T built 70 years ago as a Worsdell compound. The Carlisle line goes straight ahead and the main line turns sharp left through the roof of a building, with more tracks and platforms visible below. The explanation of this eccentricity is that the Forth goods station was built in 1871 and, when it was found to be in the way in 1906, they merely removed some of the roof trusses and roughly screened-in the gap. Still moving slowly, *Mallard* leads her coaches out onto the King Edward Bridge, the approach curves so sharp that passengers who bother to look out of the windows get a view of the engine at both ends. The design and construction of the bridge was contracted to the Cleveland Bridge & Engineering Co, it has four steel spans and is 383yd long. The view from on top is impressive but hardly beautiful, yet there is a humanity in its untidiness which would be lost if well-meaning planners cleared it all up.

As soon as the tail of the train is clear of King Edward Bridge Junction the fireman opens the damper and starts shovelling. The line actually runs downhill here from a height of 108ft above the water to near sea level at Allerdene in the Team valley, giving an unexpectedly rapid acceleration. Within a couple of minutes the regulator s full open and the driver is winding the reverser back. There is no reference in this account to precise cut-off percentages, because in reality the cab controls of this engine which was intended to perform to such precise limits are not in themselves particularly precise. The cut-off is shown by a pointer on a plate about a foot long, marked 15, 25, 45, 65 and 75. The pointer

is attached at cab floor level to the rear end of the reversing rod which leads to the weigh-shaft half-way along the engine, and there are several more pin joints between that and the valve heads moving in their steam chests. The weigh-shaft is provided with a band brake actuated by a vacuum cylinder and controlled by a small handle on the reverser stand, which enables the driver to make adjustments to the cut-off as fine as he likes, but that not withstanding, the connection between the pointer and the actual valve opening is a pretty distant one. There is no guarantee that it shows what the cut-off really is, especially for the middle cylinder, and reports from footplate riders quoting cut-offs of 18% or 22% are, frankly, a lot of baloney. All that can truthfully be said is that for hard work the pointer is around the 25 mark and for cruising it is around 15. If you look at it now, for instance, as we are passing Low Fell Sidings, it is near mid gear, but the engine is still pulling very heartily indeed. Similarly, people who state steam pressures in graduations of less than 5lb are pulling the wool over your eyes there as well, as while running the gauge needle is in constant vibration. One thing we do know is how fast we are going, as *Mallard* is one of the few engines in this country fitted with a speedometer. It is a French Flaman speed recorder which originally plotted the speed on a moving strip of paper, introduced to check that drivers did not break the speed limits on the streamliners. However, even this may not be quite the authority it is cracked-up to be, as the scale is small and there are no fewer than five universal joints between the instrument and its drive from the rear coupled axle. The recording part no longer works, and indeed the instruments have been removed from most other engines altogether. It resides under the fireman's seat, so it is no use to the driver, but he is expected to judge his speed and run to time by the feel of the engine assessed through experience. Just now we are well up to the limit of 50mph.

Between Low Fell and Birtley a wavering line of rails crosses under the main line: the Pontop & Jarrow Wagonway. It is a survivor of the early wagonways constructed to bring coal down from West Durham to the coast, and although this part dates only from 1842 it is worked in the old way by rope haulage. South of Birtley is the now disused track of the Pelaw Main Wagonway and at Ouston Junction on a overbridge is the track of the infamous Stanhope & Tyne Railway. Nowadays it is known chiefly as forming part of the route from Tyne Dock to the Consett Iron Works, over which work trains of iron ore in special air-braked hopper wagons built for the job in 1951, hauled by the North Eastern 'Q7' class three-cylinder 0-8-0s. These relics of the old

Above:
A cold light at Newton Hall Junction, the year 1963. 'A3' No 60106 *Flying Fox* passes on the up fast line.
M. Dunnett

industry contrast with the Team Valley Trading Estate, spread out new, clean and bland across the valley bottom. It is rail-served from Low Fell yard, where the 8.46am goods from York is seen detaching wagons. Another freight is trundling slowly along the down goods line from Ouston, to be overtaken by the 10.5am York-Newcastle passenger train at the same moment. On the other side is the factory of Henley's of Birtley, whose own engine is shunting their sidings.

It is vital to have our steam and water up to the mark here, for *Mallard* will have to work into the collar for most of the next 20 miles. She works up to 60mph by Chester viaduct and does well to hold that on the long climb past Chester Moor and Kimblesworth collieries. The viaduct

gives us a good view of the town of Chester-le-Street, and with no disrespect intended to the people who live and work there, the prospect holds little inspiration apart from the distant Penshaw Monument on the left horizon. Better to concentrate on firing until the driver eases her for Newton Hall Junction. A sign in the field below reads 'NEWCASTLE VIA LEAMSIDE' referring to a link line from here to the old main line which passes to the east of Durham. On half throttle and 15% she takes the junction and slows to 30mph as a view opens out ahead of dramatic impact. Above the Wear valley rises the huge square tower of Durham Cathedral. This is certainly a route of fortresses and here is the most spectacular one of all; there is a castle on the same eminence, but it is quite overawed by the display of ecclesiastical dominance. As the train rides through the station and along a high viaduct the cathedral is directly opposite the carriage windows across the smoky streets of Durham City, and has even been known to cause passengers to glance up from their newspapers. Then it is hidden as we run into a cutting and punch the engine up the last pitch to Relly Mill. There is a chance to make up time here, as the permitted speed is raised to 50mph through the junction complex, 70mph to Browney and 80mph from there, so we open up the regulator and let her get on with it. The fireman is looking a little concerned, as pressure is down to 210lb. He shuts the feed off, turns the blower on and uses the fire-irons to push the fire out from the back corners into the thin front. There is a slight accumulation of ash and dirt, and we don't want it settling on the bars in solid clinker at this stage; as the lineside sign in Croxdale cutting says, there are still 250 miles to go. He then has to put a fresh fire in, and by the time he can pause for a breather she has racketed down to Croxdale viaduct and is surging up by Hett Moor.

Water is down to a couple of inches in the glass, but the driver is not worried — although he appears to be concentrating on the road he is keeping half an eye on the situation and believes she will come round all right once we are over the top at Bradbury. He keeps her going at full tilt round the corner at Tursdale, where we join the old main line, but here is another distant signal on, Coxhoe, and he shuts off and puts the brake on. Immediately his mate abandons his shovel and remains at the right-hand window, both pairs of eyes watching the junction signals nearly a mile away – a disadvantage of the 'A4' cab is that while you can fire without stooping too much, it is impossible to glance through the front window without getting up onto the seat dais, even the gauge-glasses being seven feet above the centre floor section. With speed down to 20mph, we see the relevant signal come off

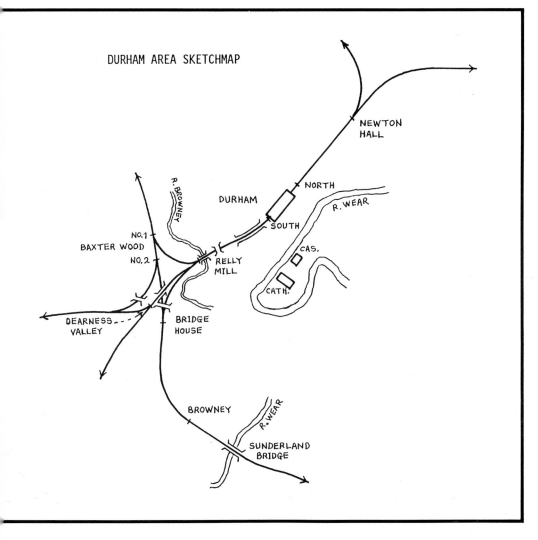

DURHAM AREA SKETCHMAP

NEWTON HALL

R. BROWNEY

DURHAM

NORTH

R. WEAR

SOUTH

NO.1

BAXTER WOOD

NO.2

RELLY MILL

CAS.

CATH.

DEARNESS VALLEY

BRIDGE HOUSE

BROWNEY

R. WEAR

SUNDERLAND BRIDGE

Looking across Durham Viaduct towards Elvet Hill on a May morning in 1963. 'K1' 2-6-0 No 62003 is drifting down to the station with a very mixed goods. Signal experts will be able to explain why the home signal and call-on arm come to be raised at the same time.
M. Dunnett

Sunday 27 August 1961 at the Relly Mill complex, with the 10.25am Waverley-King's Cross diverted off the main line, which lies down on the right. The signals show that it is heading for Darlington via Bishop Auckland. The engine, *Union of South Africa*, is carrying a headboard back to front, a usual way of keeping it with its engine. Note the pictures on the hut wall — graffiti admittedly, but what a delightful touch.
I. S. Carr

and take her past the distinctive over-line Coxhoe signal box, towards Ferryhill.

The large station here is a meeting point of several lines, but it lost most of its passenger trains in the early 1950s and has a deserted air, for although there are several quarries and mines nearby there is no major town. The extensive sidings are still busy, and in there is the train which has been preceding us along the main line — the 11.5am Low Fell-Stockton service. It should have reached here 25min ago, so it too must be running late and must have given Control some thought as to whether to allow it to continue or to hold it for us to pass at Durham. Perhaps the 'J26' is not doing too well.

At this point the first daytime train from London that we see comes past — the 7.50am to Newcastle. Again *Mallard* chatters crisply as with all signals off at Ferryhill No 3 we build up our speed. Now it is our turn to hold someone else up, for, at Darlington, the 12.30pm train to Saltburn is supposed to start as soon as we have passed and cross over the main line behind us at Croft Junction, and wouldn't it be just like those antipathetic so-and-so's of signalmen to let it go ahead in the quite erroneous belief that ours is not the most important train on the entire railway. However, a top-link driver does not abuse his engine and tear a fire to pieces just to gain a few minutes, and he bides his time, content to run a little faster than usual so that approaching Darlington we are about five minutes behind time.

Croxdale Viaduct, looking north on 5 August 1952. A 35-wagon freight is hauled by a 'V2' class engine. The first four wagons are six-wheeled flats loaded with road tank trailers. To the right the River Wear flows beneath the viaduct, and the building in the background is Burn Hall.
A. M. Bowman

This view north of Ferryhill shows a Stephenson Locomotive Society special train hauled by the lamented 'Jubilee' class engine *Alberta,* on 10 June 1967. The train is on the up main line. Behind are the metals of the old main line to Penshaw and the freight line to Bishop Auckland, which rises in the distance towards Coxhoe Junction. Above the rear of the train, much overgrown, are sidings serving Thrislington Colliery. Above the engine are some hopper wagons on sidings to the Mainsforth Lime Works and its quarry on top of the hill. A particularly impressive feature is the complexity of the telegraph rig; there are at least 86 insulators on the two pole lines.
J. M. Boyes

Happily we have plenty of steam once more, indeed she is coming round against the injector and the fireman puts the other one on to prevent her from blowing off.

Near Preston le Skerne a line crosses over ours which is not only a pioneer railway, the Clarence, but was an early example of main line electrification; from 1915 to 1934 it carried electric coal trains from Shildon to Newport-on-Tees. A more famous railway crosses the main line on the level at Parkgate Junction, north of Darling-ton: the Stockton & Darlington. *Mallard* gives a nod of recognition as she clatters over this historic spot, for although it was not in fact the first to do anything, the S&D was where all the elements of railway transport as we now understand it were brought together for the first time. Nowadays when all the talk is of 'Modernisation' it is fashionable to deride the pioneers as merely proving how clever we are in comparison, but all our fast cars and jet airliners are only enlargements in scale of the idea of linking communities by fast powered transport, and it began here. The plain notice, reading 'STOCKTON AND DARLINGTON RAILWAY 1825' planted in a run-down industrial landscape, is arguably the most important single monument in our civilisation.

On the northern approach to Darlington we pass several notable homes of heavy industry. Foremost among them is the Springfield Works of Robert Stephenson & Hawthorn Ltd, on the east side at Parkgate, and nearby are the Darlington Forge, Darlington Wire Mills and the Cleveland Bridge & Engineering Co. The railway works lie half a mile to the west along the S&D line. Further on to our left is the locomotive depot and to the right Bank Top station, concealed in its single huge overall roof. Through lines take us past it, and amazingly they are actually laid on a straight alignment, allowing us to go through at full speed. Everything is stopped to let us pass including a freight on the down side, the 2.48am from Normanton, hauled by one of the unloved Austerity 2-8-0s, waiting to pull in to the sidings at Croft Junction. We are now running at nearly 70mph and are entering on the famous racing stretch, but before going off on a glorious dash it would be as well to remember the water supply. There is not much more than 1,000gal in the tender, so the pick-up from Wiske Moor trough is the highest priority, and hard running could easily make up the lost time but could let us in for a problem later on. We are not really badly off for water, though, as the boiler is full, and although pressure is on the red line the driver signals his mate to shut off the injectors; in his determination to keep her quiet he has overdone it a little and the water is at the top of the glass now. We have been running on half regulator for some distance and opening it fully causes the boiler water level to rise, with a risk of carrying water over with the steam if it is too high. Moments later there is a shattering roar above our heads. The two safety valves are on top of the firebox and are enclosed by the V-shaped front of the cab roof, so when they lift some of the noise is kept in the cab with us and leaves us in no doubt at all that they are open. Although they are both set to lift at 250lb, one is bound to open first and creates a local reduction in pressure so that the other one often stays shut. It then stays open until pressure has fallen to about 245lb, but in the present case opening the engine out also pulls pressure down, so it shuts after a few seconds and we can then settle down again with 15% cut-off (or whatever it really is) and full regulator.

Leaving behind Croft Junction's sidings, the scene becomes rural as the train rushes down to Croft Spa, where the River Skerne joins with the River Tees. The latter has none of the industrial character with which we associate its lower reaches, for Croft was a health resort, promoted for its medicinal springs while such were in vogue. To sustain the level of our road there is a half-mile in cutting on the approach to the high river bridge, followed by a tremendous cutting extending for three miles. That, of course, cuts off any view other than the track ahead until we emerge into the level farmland of the Plain of York.

Below:
The railway's bread and butter — freight. 'V2' No 60884 pulling out of Darlington towards Black Banks with the 10.25am Croft Junction- York on 7 April 1965, near the end of her career.
M. S. Burns

Above:
A close-up on Wiske Moor troughs, *Silver King*, one of the original 'silver' quartet, on the up 'Flying Scotsman' on 26 August 1947. The absence of spray from the train, the low water level in the near trough and the presence of the fitters imply that the troughs were out of use at the time. The first vehicle in the train is a standard bogie brake.
E. R. Wethersett/IAL

By now conditions on the footplate are becoming a bit dusty, as you might expect after some three tons of coal have passed through it in three hours. Above the tender shovel plate an inward-opening door is provided, and once the coal heap is clear of it the fireman opens it. He uses the hose-pipe fitted on the boiler backhead to spray the coal and wash down the tender front and cab floor, then he fills a bucket which is stowed in a hole in the floor on the driver's side with a tap above it, and washes his hands and face. Before long, however, he resumes firing: bend, lift, turn and throw, still with an ease and economy of effort acquired through years of practice. He is reminded of the approach of the water trough by the driver easing her at Danby Wiske station. The optimum speed for scooping water is variously considered to be something between 45 and 60mph, although on our schedule we are obviously expected to be at the top limit, and will be over the trough for just 21sec. Getting the scoop down and up to make the most of that time takes a cool nerve and strong arms, and incidentally it is a fair piece of engineering which will hinge down and withstand the impact of a flow rate, expressed in the conventional term, of over 6,000gal per minute. This pick-up marks the end of the third hour of our journey.

As a result of widening works prosecuted over many years there are four tracks all the way from Wiske Moor to Church Fenton, south of York on the Leeds line, except for the Pilmoor-Alne section where there is no up slow, and running goods loops from Eryholme Junction to Cowton. During our passage from Darlington to York we are due to pass 13 timetabled down trains, if the 'Norseman' to Tyne Commission Quay is running, not including extras. One of them is the down 'Elizabethan', the theoretical crossing point being at Sessay station, although as we are behind time it will probably be nearer Thirsk. The up 'Elizabethan' is due to overtake two trains, the 12.39pm Northallerton-Leeds, which turns off the main line at Thirsk, and the 11.0am Newcastle-Leeds, which should be making its stop at Thirsk when we go through. That is a good place to watch trains at this time of day, for it has a pilot engine on duty, and a cross-country freight — the 9.0am Skipton-Newport service — is shunting there meanwhile, whilst the 11.30am Leeds-Newcastle is booked to pass at the same moment. (That train stops at Northallerton, there to wait until the down 'Non-Stop' has overtaken it.) The only direct effect all these movements have on us is to prompt prolonged use of the whistle at Otterington and Thirsk, as both station platforms will be crowded with passengers. With colour-light signals clearly visible far along the straight track, there is no hindrance to giving the engine free reign to show us what she can do. Gradually speed rises – past 80mph. A piece of flat country gives you the feeling that the world is a big place, when even the full power of an 'A4' doesn't seem to translate us very noticeably; no matter how fast the signal posts and bridges flick by, the line still stretches unwavering in front, and we have to look over to the distant Hambleton Hills on the left to be reassured that we are getting somewhere. 90mph on the level!

Into the Ridings

Thirsk station, over a mile from the town, is not a name that springs to mind as a tourist venue, even in the period when James Herriot's stories set in the district were accorded cult status, but in the early 1930s railway managers from all over the world were going there. In 1931 it was equipped with what was then the most advanced signalling installation in the world. Everything was electric, the signalmen viewed trains on an illuminated panel and controlled them by pushing buttons, and safety systems were automatic and foolproof. This state-of-the-art showpiece attracted a stream of admirers and it also acquired a ghost train. The story was told to us by Mr Woods, stationmaster, of how one stormy day they were struck by lightning. Of course, they had an emergency power supply from a standby generator which could be switched in immediately to the mains supply cable. The cable was where the thunderbolt hit. Off went lights, power, heating, signal lamps, point machines, track circuits, telegraphs, telephones – the lot. Having been rendered at a stroke deaf, dumb and blind with respect to the rest of the railway, the staff were wondering what to do next when a train appeared: an express hauled by one of the latest Pacifics. It roared through the station at full speed and out through all the blank signals, and they never discovered from whence

Below:
The premier mixed-traffic engines in the York area are the North Eastern 'B16s'. No 61472 is running through Thirsk on the up slow on 24 March 1953. Over six years after the mines were nationalised, the third wagon still bears its former owner's name.
J. W. Hague

it came or whither it went. Is it still on the road in some other dimension?

Technical hitches notwithstanding, within a couple of years the new system was being spread along the route, financed largely from the public purse by the Loans & Guarantees Act, and now all of Darlington to York is controlled by automatic colour-light signals. Signalboxes exist at Croft Spa, Black Banks, Cowton, Danby Wiske, Wiske Moor, Castle Hills, Otterington, Sessay, Pilmoor, Raskelf, Tollerton and Beningbrough, but they are only manned when needed for local operations and the signals work by themselves most of the time, controlled by track circuits. The basis of the track circuit is simply an electric current flowing through a relay coil. At each end of the relay is a connection to one rail of an isolated length of track. If a train runs onto the track its wheels bypass the coil, steal the current from it and de-energise it — as would a failure of the electricity supply. The relay switches a signal to Danger behind the train, and a string of them along the line are interconnected to clear that signal as the train moves away. The same principle can be used to interlock points and indicate the positions of trains in a remote control room.'

Having reduced the power and speed of the 'Non-Stop' to the status of a few winking lights on a control panel, we return to the train to find that most of its passengers, too, are taking their progress along the Plain of York pretty much for granted. At one end of the third-class dining area, quietly finishing their meal, are two men, unremarkable except in seeming to be immune to the swings and lurches of the coach. Without speaking they make their way to the front of the train; in the end compartment they don overalls and grease-top hats and one produces an item not usually needed by enginemen: a No 1 key for coachend doors. At the far end of the baggage van he opens the wooden sliding door and a green metal door beyond that, and steps from he walnut veneer and soft lighting to a cavern of naked metal, roaring and resounding to the pulse of the beast in front. Much of the noise comes from a metal ladder lying on the floor, over which he has to step, keeping his head well down and his shoulders braced against the side of the jerking, swaying tunnel. Gaining the footplate, he crosses over and taps the Haymarket driver on the shoulder. The latter slips off the seat and the King's Cross man instantly takes his place. The firemen exchange a few words about how the engine is doing. Before he follows his mate through the tender the Haymarket fireman attends to his face, carefully applying a big mudge of coal-dust to his forehead and down one cheek. The reason for this you will see if you follow him back into the train: with the addition of a wetted dirty handkerchief round the neck, by the time he reaches the buffet car the transformation from cool professional to grimy, muscle-weary hero is complete. The buffet attendant will play along by suddenly shouting: 'Here they are,

ladies and gentlemen, the crew who have brought us from Scotland and have just come off the locomotive at 90 miles an hour!' And it is a poor day if someone does not stand him a cup of tea at the very least.

Meanwhile at the sharp end, the new fireman takes stock of the situation. It is quite true that we are still doing 90mph; pressure is 220lb with half a glass of water and a good white fire. There is little demand for steam right now and won't be for a while with the slow passage of York to come, so he can start a fairly leisurely build-up of the fire he will want for pulling away after the slowing. While this is going on our wheels are casting astern that quaint byway the Easingwold Railway at Alne, and the half-way point, marked by a curious metal sculpture, near a house called Newton Grange about 1½ miles south of Tollerton station, in sight of the big airfield of Linton on Ouse. The last few miles of the racing stretch whirl away until the regulator is shut, the brake applied, and ahead, rising in serene majesty, appear the towers of York Minster.

Before the factory system was adopted in industry, towns grew up not to house concentrations of workers but to serve conjunctions of travellers. It follows that the factors which confirmed our ancient towns as crossroads also made them railway centres, and this is nowhere better seen than at York, where the railways

Below:
The 1930s colour-light signals are prominent in this view of the 'Non-Stop' heading north on the last day of the 1953 season, 12 September. It is passing the triangular junction at Pilmoor with the Malton line behind it.
. W. Hague

Above:
Inside the tender corridor pictured as the relief crew see it as they pass through to the footplate. This view is in tender No 5324, running with *Sir Nigel Gresley,* in October 1992.
SHA

cover about the same area as the old walled city. Most of it is occupied by goods sidings and warehouses never seen by the travelling public, so the accompanying diagram covers only the tracks through the passenger station. The original station, which still exists, is the YNM terminus within the city walls. When the GNE line came from the north to intersect it at right angles, not only was there no room for expansion but it could not be used by through trains without reversing; hence the present station on a loop line turning through fully 150°. To walk through the entrance hall into the centre of its great curved arches is a breathtaking experience that leaves one in no doubt that this is one of the

Right:
The half-way sign may be regarded as a piece of art deco and we would not like to see it go, but it is hardly a thing of beauty.
British Railways

noblest pieces of architecture in the land. It has 16 platforms of which the longest, No 8, is 540yd long. From the new platform on the inside of the curve can be seen two other huge railway buildings, the North locomotive depot, containing four turntables under one roof, and the main goods shed. To the west are two more locomotive roundhouses, one now roofless, the smaller Midland engine shed, and beyond the Branches yard the wagon repair works. Away on the far side of the goods lines is York Carriage Works. Even this vast complex proved inadequate in time, and marshalling yards were built at Skelton to the north and Dringhouses to the south. There is always something moving somewhere: at midday there are in the area 21 shunting engines at work, seven in the main yards, two for the goods shed, one in Branches yard, one at Clifton, four in the station, four in Dringhouses and two on general trips.

Following the success of power signalling on the main line, the LNER engineers naturally wanted to tackle the big one – York itself — but, although work started in 1937, the war interrupted and it was not finished until 1951. The scheme covers 33 miles of track, with 277 electro-pneumatic points and 341 signals, controlled from a central signalbox. Operation is by route

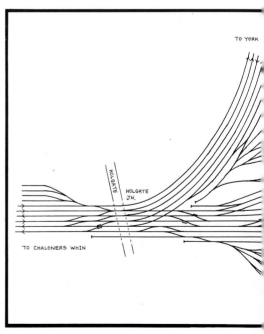

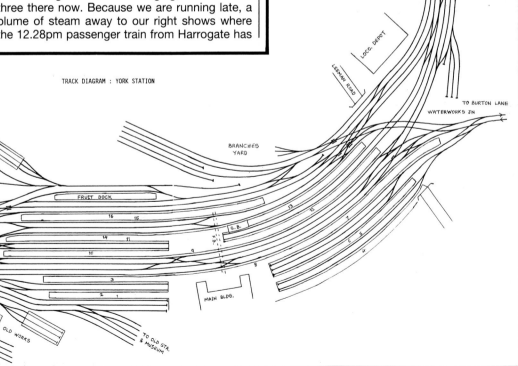

TRACK DIAGRAM : YORK STATION

setting, in which one switch moves all the points and clears all the signals for a train movement, thus enabling the entire layout to be worked by four signalmen, with the aid of over 3,000 relays. Making any route through the station takes just nine seconds. The whole installation is the largest of its kind in the world.

Running in from the north, the first part of the complex we come to is Skelton New Yard. Here many through goods trains pull in for examination and engine- or crew-changing, and there are three there now. Because we are running late, a plume of steam away to our right shows where the 12.28pm passenger train from Harrogate has

71

Along the Plain of York, 'V2' No 60839 with an up Sunday extra comprising 12 LMSR coaches and one, the second, a GWR coach, on 6 August 1961. It has just passed Beningbrough; Shipton village is in the background.
G. W. Morrison

We hope readers will excuse the diesel locomotive in this picture, as it was taken from the York coaling tower and shows the extent of the shed yard, with the Minster dominating the city across the river. There are at least two dozen engines in this comparatively empty scene, although the only ones clearly seen are a 'WD' 2-8-0, an 'A3' and a 'Britannia' screwed down on the ashpit in the middle. The diesel is passing the shunting neck of Clifton carriage depot.
C. P. Walker

been brought to a stand outside the junction. The goods lines go straight on but the main line turns left towards the prominent tower of an engine coaling plant. Still slowing down, we exchange greetings with the men on an 'A4', getting away with the 9.35am King's Cross-Newcastle, and pass Clifton Carriage depot on the left and the locomotive yard on our right. The display of power here is one of the great sights of British industry, whether viewed as weight of machinery, capital value or haulage capability

and while one should not belittle the hardworking occupants of the North Eastern Region headquarters or the railway laundry, it is to those lines of engines we look as representing the greatness of this institution. By the Waterworks we are down to 25mph (the limit is 15mph for all other routes) and head into the great roof on the up through road between Platforms Nos 8 and 9. Our driver sounds the whistle, partly for the sheer pleasure of hearing it raise the echoes, and starts easing the regulator open, winding the reverser down to 45%. It is just past 1.10pm, so we have run the 44 miles from Darlington in 35min at an average speed of 75mph.

Life on the footplate settles down to a now familiar routine on the way out of York, under Holgate Bridge past the cattle dock. The fireman knows his mate's habits, so he remains in his seat until the latter has whipped the 'A4' up to 50mph and pulled the lever up, reducing a draught that would suck coal off the shovel before he could put it where he wanted. Then he

The north end of York station, seem from an engine approaching the outside platform, No 16. The larger arch covers the four-road section. This view was taken in 1979 when much of the trackwork had already gone.
E. W. J. Crawforth

Left:
York station interior.
SHA

gets down into the hold and fires a couple of rounds, pausing to catch the signal at Chaloners Whin Junction. There used to be a box here, but the points and signals are now worked from York and the next signal at Bishopthorpe Lane is controlled by Naburn, the next box south. The signalman here has an excellent prospect, as he is perched high above the flat country on top of a swing bridge across the Yorkshire Ouse, an important navigable river. Presumably, if he looks

Below:
Looking through the centre of York station in the up direction, with Platform No 8 on the left and *Union of South Africa*, standing at Platform No 9. This view was taken in 1984 and the arrangement of crossovers on the through roads was different from that shown in the diagram.
K. J. C. Jackson

out of his window and sees a boat instead of a train he knows the bridge is open.

At a generous approximation to the 55mph limit the junction curve looks quite acute, but it has a steep 'cant' to it and *Mallard* swings into it smoothly. Another 'A4' appears ahead, this one hauling the down 10am 'Flying Scotsman', followed only a few minutes later by an 'A3' on the 7.20am Colchester-Newcastle. The fireman comes over to the left-hand cab-door and looks back down the train. According to Rule 143 a fireman should look back to see that the train is following all right, but the wide tender makes this difficult without running the risk of leaning outside the loading gauge, so he takes advantage of curves to check behind when he can in comfort. Then he gets to work, for this driver does not believe in hanging about when there is time to be regained. He has to ease off almost at once to observe the 60mph limit over Naburn Bridge, but puts her to it again until slowing again for progressive restrictions to 50mph at Barlby North, 50mph at Barlby and 40mph at Selby. The scene at Selby is dominated by the huge warehouses

By 1964 when this picture was taken the huge mill at Selby had been taken over by the Rank group. The train is a special, drawn by 'Black 5' No 45437, which has come off the Hull & Selby line and is now coasting down to the swing bridge on the up main line before heading for Leeds, on 8 August. Its coaches are a co-operative: a BR Standard, an LMSR Stanier, an LNER Thompson; and a Gresley bringing up the rear.
Ian Allan Library

and mills of Fawcett's, Kirby's and the British Oil & Cake Mills, through which the main line runs in a long reverse bend. They are here because this was the tidal limit of the Ouse and hence the transhipment point between sea and river craft, and also the terminus of one of the oldest railways, the Leeds & Selby, opened in September 1834. Selby has another swing bridge, better known because it adjoins the station and a main road. It can be a major interference with the timetable, because tides cannot be stopped and on occasion boats have to be given precedence over trains. (As late as 1983 the writer was on a high speed diesel train which was stopped for some time because the bridge was open when it arrived.) A curious feature of the bridge is that there are points to running loop lines to the north but the span is only two tracks wide, the signalbox that controls them is on the south side and

operating rods cannot easily be run across the gap. To deal with the problem the switches are on the south side and the two pairs of rails are interlaced across the bridge, diverging on the far side.

There is a terrific rumbling and shaking as we go through the bridge and on the centre road through the station, and in front of us is a train from Leeds standing in the down platform while an 'A4' shoots through the gap – the 10.5am 'Scotsman' relief. Then we are swinging round to head south again, past sidings where a Great Central 2-8-0 is blowing off at the head of a goods which is due to follow us as soon as we clear the section.

Another potential hazard hereabouts is that there are nine road level crossings between Selby and Doncaster, plus various uncontrolled or indeed unofficial crossing places. Given the totally flat terrain that is understandable, for the builders would have seen the expense of building bridges as unnecessary and they could not have foreseen the growth of traffic to come, but the combination of motorists careering along

The Selby swing bridge, swung. One end of the railway is on the extreme left, the other is behind the span on the right. Naburn bridge was similar. This view was taken on 12 April 1981.
J. E. Oxley

every country lane and more, faster trains promised by the Modernisation Plan is one about which sooner or later something will have to be done. It is thanks to the unsung heroes who keep these gates that our train, like most others, receives clear passage through them all, and with a permitted speed of 80mph we have every chance of getting back on time. The driver evidently thinks so as he is checking his watch and driving the engine in a positive way instead of just letting her make her own way along, experimenting with throttle and lever to find the best acceleration for the least noise. But, at the wayside block post of Moss, here is a distant signal on, and it looks like trouble.

There could be a number of causes of a hold-up at Doncaster. At Marshgate Junction main lines to Leeds and Hull diverge and, until six years ago, it was a crucial bottleneck, with a double-track bridge over the River Don; the bridge has now been rebuilt with six tracks. It could be that the train preceding us, the 11.50am Skelton-Whitemoor goods, is behind time and is being turned into Arksey loop one section ahead. The engines making their way from Doncaster Carr Loco to the station to take on the Bradford and Hull portions of the 10.18am from King's Cross have to cross our path and could be late, or we could get mixed up with another light engine going into Bentley Colliery to collect a load of coal for Crofton Power Station, due out at 1.40pm. A shunting movement could have taken longer then expected. The 7.50am Clarence Yard-Hull goods could have been put across the junction in front of us, which would be a mistake, but even Controllers can make mistakes. Whatever it is, there is no question of compromising safety and if the line is not clear then the 'Non-Stop', now passing Joan Croft Junction, will be stopped. As soon as he sees the signal the driver shuts off and flicks the blower on a little to prevent flames shooting out of the firehole when the exhaust blast ceases, then put the brake handle down. His mate turns off the exhaust injector and they both watch ahead for the home. It is off, but we play it canny and just let her roll until we sight the Shaftholme distant, and sure enough that is on too. On goes the brake again and this time the fireman shuts the ashpan damper and starts up the live-steam

Above:
Mallard **herself cruising through Doncaster with the up 'Northumbrian' on 23 May 1959, the day when *Sir Nigel Gresley* ran the first train advertised to do 100mph. The perfectly clear exhaust shows that the fireman has her well under control, although the job is not too arduous with just eight BR Standards and a Gresley restaurant first.**
P. J. Kelley

injector. Down to 30mph. It feels like a slow crawl, and gives us a chance to view the scenery, which hereabouts consists mainly of fields interspersed with scrubby trees and sluggish drainage ditches. This is what Edmund Denison had in mind when he made his remark about his Great Northern Railway ending in a ploughed field four miles north of Doncaster, although the spot he was referring to is about a mile to the west at Askern, where the infant GN linked up with a branch of the York & North Midland from Knottingley. That route joins the line we are on at Shaftholme.

Arksey distant is on, we are ready to stop at the now closed station, and there is the tail end of the goods train. We give a long whistle, not as an expression of annoyance but to warn anyone who might be on the ground around that train that we are coming past them. Impatience plays no part in railway operation nor in an engineman's approach to the job; while we would prefer to avoid stopping, if it happens, it happens and that's that. Another brake application as Bentley Colliery passes abeam brings her down to 20mph. Boiler water level, which of course we have not forgotten, is rising inexorably to the top of the glass and now there is no choice but to turn the injector off. Moments later the safety valves lift. There is nothing we can do about it, so we might as well ignore it, in so far as it is possible to ignore that screeching roar, but it brings to the fore another consideration — water. Consultation of the water gauge shows that there is less than 1,000gal in the tank, and if the delay is a long one it might be prudent to have Doncaster North turn us into the station platform road to stop and fill up. This request would be conveyed by sounding a series of quick pops on the whistle while approaching Marshgate.

The driver brakes her down again to a fast walking pace and leaves his seat to have a look at the water state for himself. He looks ahead again. Blowing-off ceases abruptly, leaving a silence unbelievable after the battering of noise and vibration we have been enduring for so long; she is drifting across Bentley Ings towards the overbridge of the former Great Central by-pass line.

'If they give us the road we'll go on through. Leave the injector off.'

At that moment the Marshgate signals move to clear. Satisfaction is evident by an exchange of nods as he pulls open the regulator. For all the avowals that it doesn't matter, it is nice to know that we have not yet stopped.

Before the railway came, Doncaster was an agricultural market town, situated on the Great North Road and the navigable limit of the River Don. Heavy industry did not reach it until late, because the coal measures slope downwards from west to east and only in the mid-19th century did attempts begin to reach them in this area. Bentley pit, for instance, took three years to sink and began raising coal in 1908 from a depth of 1,800ft. Markham Main came in in 1924 and Thorne in 1925. The spur was of course demand: most of the coal goes for electricity generation in power stations like Ferrybridge and Drax, which have been prominent on our skyline, one each side, for many miles back. The railway works, known to everyone as 'The Plant', was established in 1853 and built their first locomotive in 1867. The long building with a clock tower at one end which we see from the station is now given over to carriage building and repair; the birthplace of *Mallard* and many other stars of the iron way is the Crimpsall, further to the west, opened in 1901. During its heyday in the 1930s this shop produced locomotives of unparalleled excellence, but in the postwar climate the engineering industry is being asked not for ingenuity and craftsmanship but for off-the-shelf cheapness; here as elsewhere the glory has departed. The only new locomotives built in recent years are some British Railways' Standard 2-6-0s and they are destined to be the last steam locomotives built here.

When the railway was built, south of the town stretched nothing but marshes, or carrs, unexploited except for wildfowl traps, or decoys. Hence the names of the signalboxes dotted among the yards and junctions which now cover the area. The GNR may have been a newcomer on the railway scene, but it was certainly no laggard in working up its business, as the vast mileage of sidings here bears witness. The marshes may also have provided the inspiration

Below:
A typical train of the South Yorkshire area, a load of coal hauled by Great Central 2-8-0 No 63693 in August 1960. It is entering Doncaster station, under North Bridge and past the signal which might have diverted us into the platform road.
J. C. Baker

79

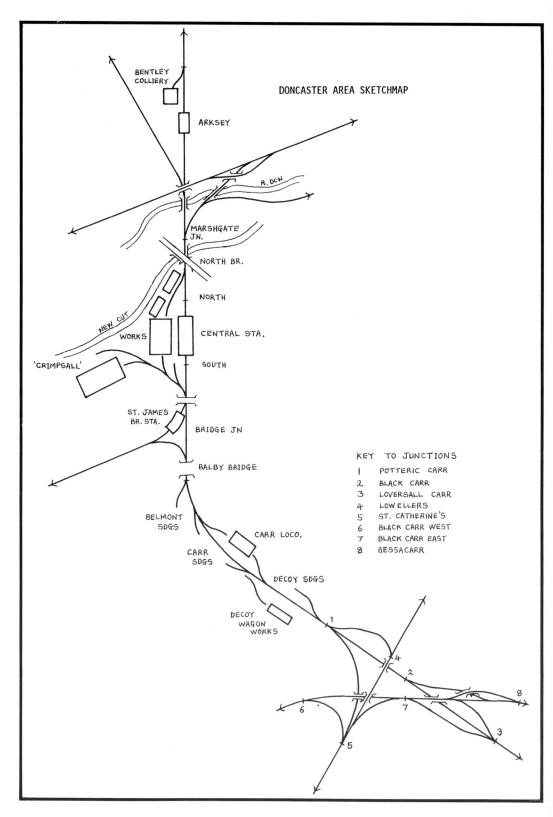

DONCASTER AREA SKETCHMAP

KEY TO JUNCTIONS

1 POTTERIC CARR
2 BLACK CARR
3 LOVERSALL CARR
4 LOWELLERS
5 ST. CATHERINE'S
6 BLACK CARR WEST
7 BLACK CARR EAST
8 BESSACARR

for the bird names on the 'A4' class engines: they are generally said to be symbolic of grace, power and speed, but it is possible that to the directors and their well-to-do patrons they would more immediately suggest sport and something that can be shot and eaten.

There is a good deal of whistling as we run into Doncaster Central station, as two engines are facing us, an 'A3' and a 'Shire', one on the Bradford train by the platform and one on the centre road, and they are given the standard hand gesture, understood by all enginemen. The platform canopies are unusual in being supported on columns between the centre roads and platform roads, leaving a narrow way between which becomes very noisy when Mallard's safety valves lift again, and as we pass under the Balby Road bridge the sound hits us like a blow and we cannot see each other for steam. Comparative quiet returns as, on full regulator once more, she accelerates through the sidings and stops blowing-off. Someone else is giving us a salute on their whistle which is clearly derisory; it is the crew on a 2-8-0 waiting to get away from Decoy yard with the 1.50pm to York.

Truth to tell, there could be just a trace of bloody-mindedness in the driver's decision to eschew a water stop, for he knows that there is a temporary 30mph restriction through Bawtry, which leaves barely half a mile to get up speed before Scrooby trough. The Powers That Be are satisfied that this is adequate, but they don't have to drive the trains. Pulling away out of the carrs, here is the first appreciable gradient we have encountered for 80 miles, over a minor summit at Rossington Hall. Incidentally, at this point the line dodges over the Yorkshire border, and at the viaduct it finally leaves the county we entered at Croft an hour and a quarter ago. He gives the brake a rub on the drop down towards Bawtry, and glances round at the fireman thoughtfully trying the tender tap. Nothing comes out. 'You'll have to piss in it!'

She rolls steadily down past the station. Viaducts are especially vulnerable to subsidence in mining districts and Bawtry has had, and will go on having, its share of problems. The speed limit was to become more or less permanent into the diesel era. It probably isn't doing the nearby church any good either. As the end of the viaduct approaches he winds the reverser to 45% and pulls the regulator open as far as it will go. The effect is shattering. You can actually feel the surge forward and the whirls of dust on the floor are being pulled up by the raging blast that at the front end is putting what looks like flames out of the chimney top. 40mph, 50mph, the trough is coming up, stand by to put the scoop down. As the usual cloud of spray erupts each side he calms that unbridled charge, keeping her on 25% to overcome the drag of the scoop, then bringing it back to 15%. This trough is 700yd long, extending almost as far as Scrooby station, whose users if any must be accustomed to southbound trains bringing a private rainstorm in with them. I say 'if any' because the down train passing now, the 12.42pm Grantham-Doncaster local, does not stop there, although there is goods traffic and our meteoric approach is enjoyed by the men on an engine which is making ready for an up working. We have picked up a good 2,000gal, so we are all set. The exhaust injector is singing, some fast stoking is repairing our summarily depleted fire, and speed is once more rising toward the 80mph. The time is five past two, so we are about nine minutes late. Chase those minutes across Barnby Moor, up the rise from Botany Bay box to the bridge over the Chesterfield Canal.

Towards the Home Counties

Speed should be reduced to 65mph at Retford, which has another level crossing; not a moribund mineral line here but the double-track Great Central main line. The castanet rattle as our wheels hit the right-angle crossing is terrific. Ahead three up goods trains are being pulled off the main line to await our pleasure: the 1.20 pm Doncaster-New England, which has been looped at Grove Road box; the 12.45pm Doncaster-Colwick, at Egmanton; and the 7.35am Doncaster-Grantham, which is a local, now arriving at Claypole. The countryside hereabouts is again agricultural, a pastoral scene of gently rising lands, hardly meriting the description of hills but undulating enough to give us a 1 in 200 climb to a summit at the curious little tunnel, only 57yd long, of Askham. This is the district known as The Dukeries, because most of it was owned by some very powerful members of the nobility, including the Duke of Norfolk, the Duke of Port-

and, Lord Savile and Earl Manvers. Here they could enjoy their country seats in rolling parkland, out of sight of the sordid industry that brought them their wealth. Small wonder that a railway promoted to carry coal was not welcomed. In this egalitarian age, retinues of servants and hunters are no longer unloaded at feudal country stations, and in fact Tuxford North has just been closed, partly because it lies less than a mile from the two-level interchange station of Dukeries Junction where the Lancashire, Derbyshire & East Coast line crosses over. This summit section we traverse at about 65mph and the descent towards the River Trent sees another 80mph past Crow Park. Having put his fire in order, our fireman has a sit-down and a quick cup of tea before it is time to take up more water from the second of the closely spaced pair of troughs, at Trent (or Muskham). As always he watches the road in between whiles, looking out for level crossings, for there is another plethora of them along here: Markham, Tuxford, Egmanton, Grassthorpe, Carlton, Cromwell, Bathley Lane, North and South Muskham. In this flat country the most conspicuous landmarks are the church spires, Carlton on Trent on the left and South Muskham on the right being particularly noticeable.

Inspection of the water level after the Trent pick-up shows that it did not lift as much as it should have done, perhaps because we might have been going a little too fast. We have about 3,000gal on board, which should be adequate with an economical engine like this one, and there is still a goodly pile of coal left, perhaps 4 tons, with 125 miles to go and an hour and 55min to do it.

Newark is a country market town, as are Retford and Grantham, although in ancient times it was fought over by Romans, Danes, Saxons, and so on, occupying as it does an important position on the Fosse Way. (Place-names ending in -by or -thorpe are of Danish origin, whereas -ham is Anglo-Saxon.) Its industries are agriculturally-based, such as Branston Maltings and British Glues & Chemicals, different from the coalfields but with a savour of their own on a hot day. By now passengers who have enjoyed their lunch may be settling for a doze, but they are momentarily disturbed by a rumble from the Trent bridge and another thump as the train goes over a third level rail crossing. A curiosity about this one is that in the bad old pre-nationalisation days the crossing itself was the property of the Midland Railway, and later of the LMSR; so for over a century the East Coast route functioned by courtesy of a rival concern.

The line now leaves the Trent meadows on a 16-mile climb into arable country. Firing is almost continuous and the driver is pushing her along at nearly 70mph, which is really an exceptional performance although one begins to take it for granted after hours of high speed. On a long period of constant effort such as this the injector can be set to keep the water level constant in the glass and a skilled and experienced fireman can feed the fire at the same rate as it is burning away, and then if the engine and boiler are well-proportioned there should be a speed at which

Left:
Silver Fox, star of the 'Elizabethan' film, carried a pair of silver foxes. Here she is going well past Retford with the up 'Norseman' boat train on 23 August 1952. The fireman looks very cheerful and is obviously taking a break after some heavy shovelling.
T. Lewis

Above:
A view south from South Muskham level crossing, along the water troughs towards Trent. The sign 'Spring Points' refers to the switches, which are sprung to lie in the position shown and have no operating mechanism. Anyone wishing to move over them away from the camera would have to bring his own lever.
Mrs A. Hatherill

the steam pressure also stays constant. That is a theoretical ideal of course, disregarding all the realities of wind and weather, coal and combustion, signal sighting, and indeed human fatigue. The fireman has been in action for an hour and a half and is beginning to flag a little and to look forward to easing off during the run down into Peterborough.

Soon after 2.30pm we pass at speed the 12.18pm King's Cross-Newcastle express, visible for some distance ahead as its engine, fresh on at Grantham, has a green fire making an impressive smokescreen, and pass Barkston, crossing above the Great Northern Nottingham-Lincoln line. What gave the junction here a niche in history was that it is a triangle and was used for turning the trains on the 1938 brake trials; so it was here that *Mallard* started her record run. Soon after we enter Peascliffe Tunnel (967yd);

with the engine working hard we are enveloped in steam and the throat-catching smell of Yorkshire coal, darkness invading our cab as far as the illuminated centre where the fireman is unconcernedly plying his shovel, a living darkness pulsating to the exhaust beat and flinging our whistle back into our ears. Why sound the whistle inside a tunnel? Well, every yard of track has to be inspected every day; somewhere in that smoke-filled darkness may be a man, who will need time to cross the line or retreat to one of the side refuges. Spare a thought for him, for we are only in it for half a minute but he will endure it for 20min or more, for the sake of our safe passage.

The next town, Grantham, has a unique status as a staging-post going back to the days of horse-drawn travel on the Great North Road, when it was a long day's journey from London. The tradition of changing horses persists, the horses being iron ones now, and has indeed grown since the war. Owing largely to supply shortages, the railways had to make do with any

Right:
Diving into the maw of Peascliffe Tunnel — this is actually the south end and the engine in this prewar photograph is a famous 'A3', *Papyrus*, a speed record holder in her time.
M. W. Earley

Above:
Grantham, staging-post. A splendidly turned-out 'V2'. No 60870 of Doncaster shed, moves out of a refuge siding to take over a down train.
Mrs A. Hatherill

coal they could secure and engines were being choked with slag and ash after a hundred miles' running, so a policy of changing them was adopted. There is no equivalent of Birmingham, Bristol or Bournemouth on this route, hence there is no place elsewhere quite like Grantham, where a modest station is flanked by a busy locomotive yard full of Pacifics and 'V2s'. Here we may also note that we are not the only people to be behind our time, as the 12.25pm Colwick-High Dyke mineral empties has missed its path and is standing in the distance on the Nottingham line.

All right, we know, you want to do a hundred miles an hour down Stoke Bank. You realise there is nothing magical about the figure: 101mph feels the same as 99mph and the speed indicator is far too coarsely graduated to tell exactly when you cross the line. Still, the engine is comparatively light on coal and water, and in

spite of averaging exactly 70mph from Retford we are eight minutes behind time at Grantham, so we could have a go if you will do the extra work. From the driver's side all it entails is leaving the reverser at the 25 mark, which as the pointer is known to be a bit out is probably about 30%; the work is to build and maintain a thicker fire to withstand a harder draught. You must start now, while we are heading up the valley side past the village of Great Ponton. Get down in the hole and pick up the shovel — don't grip it hard, just hold it, and don't fill it to overflowing. Lay the coal down the front of the box. Resist the temptation to toss it to get the length, as it could go anywhere: keep the shovel handle end up and drive it in fast. If your mind's eye can see the coal in the right place before you start your swing, it is halfway there. Work over the grate from sides to middle, front to back; as you come to the back corners you must turn the shovel blade over to direct the coal against the pull of the blast. And remember to keep hold of the shovel, or she'll have it out of your hands. Then start again.

Do not allow yourself to be put off by the sudden clatter as we pass a row of iron-ore wagons at High Dyke, or the throbbing darkness of Stoke Tunnel. The summit is marked by a little signal box (it happens to be 100 miles from London) and you feel the acceleration onto the 1 in 178 down. Corby Glen and 75mph, Creeton and 85mph, Little Bytham and 95mph.

Did anyone tell you to stop firing?

The engine is swaying gently and hunting a little, while rail-joints go by too fast to be noticed any more. She is now in a realm which is peculiar to the 'A4'. There is no other engine specifically designed to operate in this realm of speed, and few which can do so with the same smooth confidence. The fancy streamlining is of real value now, representing some 200hp which your muscles do not have to generate. The station that just shot by was Essendine, so you can leave off shovelling and take a look around; this is about as fast as we will go. The indicator is quivering on the 100mph mark and if you want confirmation, the time between two mileposts is just 36sec. Setting her down to 35% makes more noise but gives no increase in speed. Moreover, the injector is not keeping up with us, so either we must increase it and bring the pressure down, or she must be pulled up, and either way our speed will fall away. We will soon be at Tallington and the end of the descent, and anyway we must soon slow down for Werrington troughs.

For those who are not concentrating on speed and mileposts, there are a few points of interest on this stretch. To the west lies an area extensively quarried for iron ore and limestone, covered with a network of railways of all sorts and sizes. The outlet to the main line is at High Dyke, just north of the half-mile Stoke Tunnel. Here there will probably be a Great Northern 0-6-0 shunting or recovering its breath after bringing a load up the steeply graded branch from Woolsthorpe (birthplace of Isaac Newton). Stoke summit is the highest point on the route after Grantshouse, although for all that it is only 345ft above sea level. Down at Little Bytham another line crosses above but does not connect: the Midland & Great Northern Joint Railway. Essendine is a junction with an extensive exchange yard; over on our right an elderly Great Northern 4-4-2 tank, probably either No 67362 or No 67382 of Grantham shed, is shunting during the course of its afternoon freight working from

Below:
Coming round the bend at High Dyke sidings, where the up slow line from Grantham comes to an end, the up 'car-carrier'. The first six vehicles are Eastern Region car transporters, each loaded with six private cars, whose owners are riding in coaches behind them. The engine is once more *Silver Fox*. The date, 18 August 1962.
L. Perrin

Left:

At the south end of the High Dyke sidings, the up 'Non-Stop' passes the starter signal. This was in 1956 and the engine is *Seagull*, one of the all-time greats. Parked on the left is a train-load of iron ore.
L. Perrin

Below left:

Essendine station has no platform on the up main line; *Sir Nigel Gresley* is seen pulling away on the down main, at 1.30pm on 11 October 1958. On the back platform road is Great Northern 4-4-2T No 67398, which the photographer notes is waiting to run light to New England after duty on the Stamford branch train. The latter is in the background, now with 'N5' 0-6-2T No 69293. The marshalling yard on the right is typical of many laid down to cope with the wartime freight traffic.
P. H. Wells

Below:

The 'Non-Stop', stopped. It was pulled up on Helpston level crossing to pass a message to the signalbox, on 24 July 1961. The train is formed of BR Standard coaches with a brake composite leading, and the engine *Silver Link* was the first 'A4' built. The timber work on the crossing is absolutely pristine.
D. C. Ovenden

Stamford East. At the moment we go through the middle road an up goods, the 1.35am Newport on Tees-New England, is rattling along the slow at a breakneck 30mph, also bent on making up time. Incidentally, about two miles of the main line here is in the county of Rutland.

Now, it may have occurred to you that we have just exceeded the 90mph speed limit by a substantial margin, so readers should be reassured that it was done on a length of well-maintained, almost straight track, and was in no manner reckless. If the driver had any doubt in his mind about the condition of any yard of the permanent way he would not have considered it. Speed limits are set not only for safety but also with regard to the Engineers' capacity to make good wear and tear of the track, which latter increases with train weights and speeds, and they know perfectly well that the figures they specify are likely to be exceeded. All the same, a three-figure speed is really an extraordinary event; over three years are to pass before British Railways publicly announce a train to run at 100mph. To avoid controversy, no mention of the date or the crews' identity will be made in this account.

On drifting steam we emerge from higher ground into the Soke of Peterborough and see approaching on our right another track, the Mid-

land line, which runs parallel a few yards away, negotiating some impressive six-track level crossings. Along here was where the remarkable broadside pictures were taken for the film 'The Elizabethan Express', starring *Silver Fox*. The sequence, which includes taking water from Werrington trough, is used in several places in the film, naturally enough for it is a superb sustained view of a train at speed — something which can only be obtained from another train. Here we are over the trough, speed held down to 60mph, and before he puts the scoop down the fireman winds the handbrake on just a touch; this is said to make the tender nose down slightly and dig the scoop in deeper, although it might be just an old drivers' tale. Immediately past the trough is Werrington Junction. We have covered 20.6 miles from Stoke in 14mins at an average speed of 88mph, and have gained two minutes on the schedule. (That goods train was scheduled 47min for the same run.)

You will be pleased to see that this is not one of those railways that have a collective nervous breakdown if a boiler water level appears below the top of the gauge-glass; in fact, it is only an inch above the bottom, pressure is down to 200lb and the fire is now visible, orange and lumpy. But none of these things cause any worry. The fireman takes down the rake from its stowage on the tender front, gives her a touch of

Right:
Mallard **hauling the down 'Northumbrian' towards Walton, north of Peterborough, on 6 July 1956. Despite having at least 15 coaches on, she is running easily at a very short cut-off. In the background is the factory of Peter Brotherhood Ltd.**
D. C. Ovenden

Bottom right:
This view, on 27 July 1962, of ***Quicksilver*** **heading south on the slow line two miles north of Peterborough with a parcels train shows on the left the pick-up standards of a mail exchange apparatus on the down side. Conspicuous on the engine is the cable of the Smiths-type speedometer, mounted on the rear coupled wheel, which replaced the Flaman recorder in the 1950s. Innovations such as that and AWS were very important improvements; there is a difference between letting engineman take a pride in being able to work without such aids and forcing them to do so.**
D. C. Ovenden

Below:
Dominion of New Zealand **picking up more than enough water from Werrington trough, on an up working, on 25 July 1962. Behind the spray, a mixture of Gresley and Thompson coaches.**
D. C. Ovenden

blower and pushes the fire into a more level shape, and packs a few shovelfuls into the back corners. He sets the injector to minimum feed and in a couple of minutes both steam and water are seen to be coming slowly up as, surrounded by more railway wagons than we have ever seen in one place, *Mallard* lopes easily along until the brake is needed to bring her down for the notorious 20mph curves.

Peterborough is one of the great railway towns, a meeting place for five of the old companies, and the heart of the distribution of life-giving coal to all of eastern England. If the track in the yards were laid out in one line it would extend from London all the way to Doncaster. Approaching from the north we pass under a fly-over carrying the MGN, then on the right is Wisbech Yard and on the left New England Down Yard, with the water tower, coaling plant and buildings of New England Loco visible beyond it. Next, the vast West and East Up Yards, Westwood Junction box, opposite the Baker Perkins diesel engine factory, Westwood yard and beyond that a site being cleared for a new goods shed. Then Spital Bridge Junction with the former Midland sidings and engine shed on the right, and the engine noses abruptly left towards the North station. Still moving at about 15mph, we give her a little more steam on coming out of

the low roof, to accelerate gradually over another bend at the far end, past carriage sidings and goods depot and on up a rise towards the Nene bridge. After the vast acreage of railway property we have just seen, the station is really dreadful, a cramped, mean place with only three through roads and inadequate space for its business. Improvement plans have existed since 1935, but little was done before the war, and when the railways came under Government control they were starved of funds as a matter of policy. Perhaps one can't blame the Government for the war, but its attitude since has been a bitter blow for railwaymen who supported the socialist ideal, and after 20 years of promises they understandably view the recently announced Modernisation Plan, which will make all things new, with a deal of weary scepticism.

At this time the station area is well clogged up, as usual; the down platform is occupied by a

Below:
At the north end of Peterborough North station, *Lord Faringdon* (or *Peregrine*, as we prefer her) comes over the reverse curves on an up Leeds train on 14 October 1961. From the show of smoke we deduce that the fireman has made up his fire, and the engine is working through to London.
P. H. Wells

Above:

Union of South Africa coasting into Peterborough with the 'Junior Scotsman' 9.45am Edinburgh-King's Cross on 19 May 1961. The third coach is one of three LNER Thompson kitchen firsts. The signals behind her are clear for the main line; the train could be sent along the goods lines, signalled by the left-hand pair of arms, but that is even slower than the 20mph through the platforms. In the right background is the 1960 goods shed, and on the left skyline the coaling tower of New England locomotive depot.
P. H. Wells

diagrammed empty stock working, 11.15am King's Cross-Doncaster, its replacement engine pulling out of one of the north end bays, the other bay has a train making ready to depart for Grimsby, while outside both up and down through goods lines are also occupied by freight trains *en route* between New England and the London marshalling yard of Ferme Park. An earlier up freight, the 2.30pm, has got no further than Yaxley where it has shunted to wait for us to pass.

The scenery is now really flat. Away to the east the fen country stretches to a level horizon. The railway on this length is floating on the water-laden soil, and as we gather speed the motion of the engine is a little more uneasy. At this end of the train it is not so bad, but after the heavy engine has pushed the track down it rebounds under the lighter carriages, and at the back end there is a noticeable bounce in the ride. To the west side are the great brick-fields, miles of muddy clay pits, tall-chimneyed kilns and store sheds everywhere, served by a network of sidings extending for over five miles. From here the big firms, Fletton, Hicks, Eastwood, the London Brick Co, send trainloads all over the country, and here at least the postwar reconstruction has brought a revival.

Eventually we leave the black fens and climb away towards Leys box. Time is still being gained and the fireman is again pitching coals into a white inferno as *Mallard* rasps along at over 70mph uphill. She is still steaming freely and starts the climb with 250lb on the clock and a full boiler, a state reached by carefully managed progress all the way through Peterborough while he appeared to be giving his full attention to the signals: truly an example of a master craftsman at work. The driver is sitting relaxed and easy, but of course he has done his share of the hard graft in his time. Actually, at this point he gets down, taps his mate on the shoulder and points to the seat, and picks up the shovel himself; and for a while the two men change places.

Naturally, being over 60 he has a lot less vigour in his swing, but the dexterity in the wrist is still there and the unconscious skill that makes light work of a hard job, and this session keeps him fit.

Abbots Ripton is a small country station and for all that it is on a main line only receives five trains a day, but it is a famous name in railway history. On 21 January 1876 a coal train was being shunted, as several have been today for us, at night in a snowstorm, and because the signals that should have protected it were frozen solid in the All Clear position, two converging expresses were not warned in time. One collided with the coal train and the other, unable to stop, ploughed through the wreckage. This accident had profound effects on the way railways are worked. It subsequently became the practice to keep signals normally at Danger and only to clear them when the signalman wished to pass a train and had ascertained that the line was clear. Signals were made to fall to Danger in the event of any breakdown. Brakes on every passenger coach became compulsory. And finally, engineers began searching for a means of communication with drivers that was unaffected by weather and visibility. From the turn of the century the North Eastern part of this route was equipped with a device which, by means of a trackside trip arm, blew a whistle on the engine when passing a distant signal at Caution. Between the wars there were experiments with continuous cab-signalling, in which an on-board monitor shows the aspect of the last signal passed. Currently British Railways are developing the Hudd system (called 'Automatic Train Control' but later renamed 'Automatic Warning System'), which uses electro-magnets to transmit the signal aspects to the engine and hence needs no vulnerable moving parts on the track, and which gives both visual and audible warnings – and applies the brake if it is ignored. The Great Northern main line is the test bed for the work, and at present *Mallard* is fitted with one of the development models of the equipment although we have not had it in operation today. Close attention to 'The Elizabethan Express' film will reveal the cab control unit on *Silver Fox*, and at one point the warning siren is heard. To jump ahead a little in time, *Sir Nigel Gresley* of this class is to be the first locomotive fitted with the production version of the equipment, made by the Telephone Manufacturing Co.

On the way down towards Huntingdon the 2.10pm King's Cross-Leeds express comes by, hauled by what looks from the glimpse we have of its front view to be another 'A4'; but it is No 60700, the unique 4-6-4, currently the most powerful locomotive in Britain and a tantalising pointer to what might have been. Almost immediately after it, running on the slow line, comes a 'K3' 2-6-0 with a motley collection of vans, the 12.35pm King's Cross-York parcels. Despite the depredations of lorry cowboys, traffic in small packages is still enough to justify separate trains.

Over the summit our unofficial driver lets her rip for a minute or so, but he knows well that Huntingdon has a 70mph limit, as does Offord a little further on, so he eases off to half regulator and 15%.

The Final Stretch

As *Mallard* leans easily into the Offord curves a beautiful church lies to the left and the lovely Bedfordshire Ouse comes alongside on our right, a tranquil scene with cows, anglers, some real mallards paddling steadily along and some namesakes of another 'A4', *Wild Swan*. It does seem right that these, the swiftest steam locomotives, were named after wild birds which earthbound Man has always viewed as symbols of freedom. The steam locomotive gave us that freedom we so envied, to travel the world beyond the limitations of our own limbs. There is a paradox here, equating the rigid control and discipline of railway operation with the freedom of the wild geese, so it is superficially under-standable that some people think instead that freedom is only offered by motor cars and aircraft. Yet you need look no further than the traffic jams on the Great North Road to see the limitations of that view; and what mobility is offered to those who cannot drive a car? The train makes no such discrimination. Young or old, fit or halt, all may travel on the 'Elizabethan' and be borne over the countryside swift as birds. In its method and order it bestows a real freedom which a free-for-all will never bring.

Overhead the wild geese call from below, they are echoed, fleetingly, by the steam whistle.

In the knowledge that he has a mate who does not mind pushing things along a bit, our present driver gives her the works on the downhill to St Neots. However, in very little time she is going so fast that he has second thoughts and begins winding the reverser back until it is below the 15 mark. At nearly 90mph the engine is just purring. With whistle open she hurtles through the long sweeping curve past Sandy North, cleaving like an arrow the activity in Sandy station. Even at this speed the driver, sitting in the right-hand seat, is able to exchange gestures

Below:
The two-track bottleneck through Sandy platforms, with an up express at speed. *Merlin* looks a trifle indecorous; her whistle is askew and one of the headlamps has flipped its lid. The tracks on the far side are on a separate line, the Sandy & Potton Railway, now incorporated into the through route between Oxford and Cambridge.
J. C. Baker

with a colleague on a 'V2', standing on the down goods line with the 1.30pm long-distance goods from Clarence Yard to Niddrie waiting for another goods to clear ahead of them. Both Langford Siding and Arlesey station have goods trains in them putting off wagons — six freights in as many minutes, a demonstration of the pre-eminence of freight transport for the railways and the country. In addition there are two down passenger trains passed almost simultaneously near St Neots.

For a short time we actually have both injectors on, but this looks like a spot of vanity on the driver's part, showing the young'uns he can still do it, for she will not really stand it and he has to cut one off as the long gradient through Arlesey and Three Counties makes itself felt and his mate has to open out gradually to full regulator to keep up the momentum. Incidentally, Three Counties station is, we believe, named after the big mental asylum lying to the east, built jointly by the three counties of Bedford, Hertford and Huntingdon, and served by a short branch line. *Mallard's* purr builds to a growl and to a roar as at 75mph she swings over Cambridge Junction and through Hitchin. The 27 miles 6 chains from Huntingdon have taken us 20mins, an average of 81¼mph, and we are almost exactly on schedule at 3.37pm.

This pleasant country within reach of London was the setting for the first purpose-built 'new town', Letchworth Garden City, laid out between Hitchin and Baldock on the Cambridge line and provided with a centrally-sited station and a rail-served trading estate. (Other developers please copy.) Those who regard new towns as a recent idea may be surprised that it was founded in the year 1903.

At Stevenage summit speed is down to 70mph, and the fireman pushes the regulator down to half and relinquishes it to his mate in order to make the last pick-up from Langley trough. This done, the tender contains about 4,000gal, so the only hindrances now to a punctual arrival are likely to be traffic ones. This, the busiest part of the route, is constricted by seven tunnels and Digswell Viaduct, all accommodating only two tracks, whose widening has repeatedly been mooted and then ruled out at the mere thought of the cost. As a palliative, the Wood

Below:
On 10 March 1956, *Sir Ralph Wedgwood* is seen between Wymondley and Todd's Green, a mile from Stevenage, on an up Leeds express. The fireman is not at the cab window, he is in the middle, firing.
E. D. Bruton

Above:
A contrast in bridgework — this cast-iron footbridge near Todd's Green was known locally as the 'Halfpenny Bridge'. In the background is the bridge seen in the previous picture.
British Railways

Green-Hertford branch was extended to rejoin the main line at a dive-under junction south of Langley Troughs and provides a makeshift by-pass. Another consequence of the heavy use of this end of the line is that 85mph running comes to an end at Woolmer Green and is followed by limits of 70mph to Hatfield, 60mph to Holloway North and 40mph to King's Cross. The Controllers have the ticklish job of persuading three up trains of very different characters to coincide at Potters Bar and there reverse their order; the 3.45pm Hatfield-King's Cross local passenger, the 12.30am Inverkeithing-Ferme Park goods, and the 'Non-Stop'. To expect the goods train, which has come even further than we have, to appear spot on time is to show some faith in the railway system, and we are not surprised to see, at Cambridge Junction, two men pouring water into one end of a shapeless filthy object that, if we had time to research the matter, we might identify as an Austerity 2-8-0 on the 10.24pm

This view of *Golden Fleece* at the north end of Langley Troughs dates from between July 1948 and June 1950 and shows that Great Northern 'somersault' signal arms, pivoted at their centre, were still controlling traffic, although in the distance a down line signal has upper quadrant arms.
R. F. Dearden

Left:
'Somewhere on the Great Northern': one of that company's signals is just visible behind the steam from the 'A4' approaching. Ahead is a level crossing, with instrument hut on the left and keeper's house on the right. It has been suggested that the photographer was recording a blue or grey engine on one of the prewar streamliners, from the apparent absence of lining on the side.
C. C. E. Herbert

freight from Colwick, about a quarter of an hour late.

We press on up to Woolmer Green and then tone her down to easy steaming for the run down through Welwyn North Tunnel (1,046yd). No firing takes place in the tunnel, and with the fire-hole flap shut we have a rather more comfortable

Above:
The double line tunnels that were so vast when they were built and so restrictive soon afterwards. In the gap between Welwyn tunnels, 'B1' No 61394 is heading north into the north tunnel, on 29 September 1956.

de than last time. Into daylight in a delightfully sylvan cutting for moments only and through Welwyn South Tunnel, a mere 446yd. Out again, a clear view opens up ahead to a horizon no longer hard and summer-bright but stifled and hazy. We are approaching London.

Welwyn North station has the air of being deep in the country, with the hill at its back and overlooking Digswell. Coming towards us over the viaduct is an 'A3' working hard on a train which has uniquely become nearly as well known to the public as the passenger trains, although it is a freight: the 3pm King's Cross-Niddrie, No 66. (It is due into Niddrie Yard at 2.25 tomorrow morning.) Over the viaduct, through a cutting and past the spacious station of Welwyn Garden City, whistling up to warn anyone who might be moving around the branch goods train which has just arrived from Hertford. On our right another branch goods, the 2.0pm from Dunstable hauled by an 'N2' 0-6-2T from Hatfield shed, is trundling along an independent line which takes it into Hatfield, and we race past it. We are now 20 miles from London; in fact the Welwyn GC Corporation depot is known as Twentieth Mile Siding. Steam shut off altogether now, down through a long cutting and out over the River Lea. At this time the fireman puts a dozen shov-

elfuls of coal on the back part of the fire and then puts the shovel down. Just as working a steam engine up to its full power output is a long process, so winding it down at the end of a duty takes time and must be carried out in due order. He is now judging that he will produce enough steam to finish the run and get the engine back on the shed, ending up with a boiler full of water but the bare minimum of fire in the box. He sweeps up, disposes of all the loose coal into the fire, shuts the flap, closes the damper a bit, hoses down the floor, washes his hands and face and settles down to watch the road and finish his tea.

In Hatfield's down platform another of the local 'N2s' has arrived with a train from London and is preparing to shove it back into the carriage sidings that lie opposite the staggered up platform. The station is located in the old town, adjoining Hatfield House, seat of the Marquis of Salisbury, Prime Minister during the formative

years of the GN. A private waiting room was provided for him on the up platform — practical politics. Over to the west is a place where 20th century history has been made, the De Havilland aircraft factory. It is worth remembering that poor old war-weary Britain is still capable of leading the world: with the train we are running, for instance, and here at Hatfield with the first and still the world's only jet airliner, the Comet. It is true that this project has been clouded by tragedy, and perhaps others with more resources will improve on, and profit from, the new technology, but the achievement of the pioneers cannot be diminished and should never be derided.

On the up slow line a train of vans is going at about half our speed, probably the one from Scotland. The sides of the vehicles a few feet away make a reflecting surface and enable our crew to listen, almost subconsciously, to the sound from *Mallard's* valve gear and decide whether it is the same as it was when we started or whether any play or looseness has developed. The driver opens up to about half regulator, then pauses and looks across the plate. His mate catches his eye and nods, this minimal exchange

confirming that all is well in the steam-raising department, whereupon he gives her full throttle and she charges up the last slight up-grade past Marshmoor Siding and Brookmans Park. We shut off the injector and close the damper altogether as Potters Bar, still a country town but surrounded by new housing estates, comes in sight. Whistle up, for the local train is here, slowing to stop at the station.

If the Romans had considered the problems of railway operators they would have built London up here instead of in the Thames basin, then down trains would not have been faced with the 12-mile climb, mostly at 1 in 200, from Belle Isle to Potters Bar. As *Mallard* runs over the top and the regulator is almost shut, the water level drops to about half a glass but the steam, which was steady on 230lb, starts to rise. She dives into Potters Bar Tunnel, the longest on the route at 1,214yd. As soon as he can see the gauges the fireman starts his injector for a short time to hold pressure below the blowing-off point. A few moments later Hadley North and Hadley South tunnels, 232 and 384yd respectively, follow in

quick succession, the gap between them being largely filled by the platforms of Hadley Wood station. In the south tunnel there is a hiss from the left and the brakes begin to rub gently; the driver is thinking ahead, as usual, and is not taken by surprise when, passing Greenwood box, New Barnet distant is on. The crew stare ahead, searching the distance for that four square feet of red and white which is the sole guardian of our safe passage. The driver eases the brake handle down more, setting the brake on in good earnest. We are down below 30mph and the home signal is clearly visible 300yd ahead when he sees it swing upwards and shoves the handle up just as the fireman lifts his left hand with a shout. The latter jumps from his seat, and while the regulator is open to regain speed he takes down the straight dart and uses it to dig up the rear part of the fire and push it more level over the grate. Use of fire-irons on a hot fire is inadvisable, as ash stirred together on the bars can congeal into clinker, but his objective now as the fire thins and cools down is to keep it broken and loose to ease the labour of removing it at the end of the day.

On the embankment approaching New Barnet the built-up area closes around us, extending indefinitely ahead and engendering a feeling of claustrophobia in those of us who do not like big cities. However, beyond Oakleigh Park it is out of our sight as the train runs through a huge cutting and into Barnet Tunnel. At Cemetery an express roars by the other way with a salutation from the 'A4', the 3.50pm to Leeds, followed by a tank

Right:
More tunnels, and *Lord Faringdon* bursts out of Hadley Wood North and through the station platforms. On the down line signal on the left, the round plate is an indicator that a call plunger is provided for enginemen to remind the signalman of their presence if they are stopped there. This was in September 1952, when the 'Non-Stop' was called 'The Capitals Limited'.
J. Davenport

Bottom:
Copenhagen Tunnel filled with smoke as usual. The up line bore is just visible on the left; *Falcon* hauling the 7.55am to Cleethorpes is on the down fast line. The bridge carries the up goods line into another tunnel at a higher level on the right.
B. Morrison

engine on the down slow, on its way from King's Cross Loco to Hitchin. New Southgate is recognisable by the white buildings of the Standard Telephones & Cables factory. The fireman lifts his fire all over with the dart, levelling it out to a uniform orange, and turns on the live-steam injector. Steam is still around 240lb with half a glass of water. More braking is needed as Wood Green Tunnel swallows us.

Under a flyover carrying the Hertford Loop. The up side along past Wood Green station is lined with carriage sidings, on which several trains are standing, some with 'N2' tanks coupled to them. On the down side is a sudden open vista, leading to a hilltop and one of the best-known and loved profiles in the Home Counties — Alexandra Palace. Not another royal residence, the Palace was built in 1873 as what will come to be called a leisure centre. It later

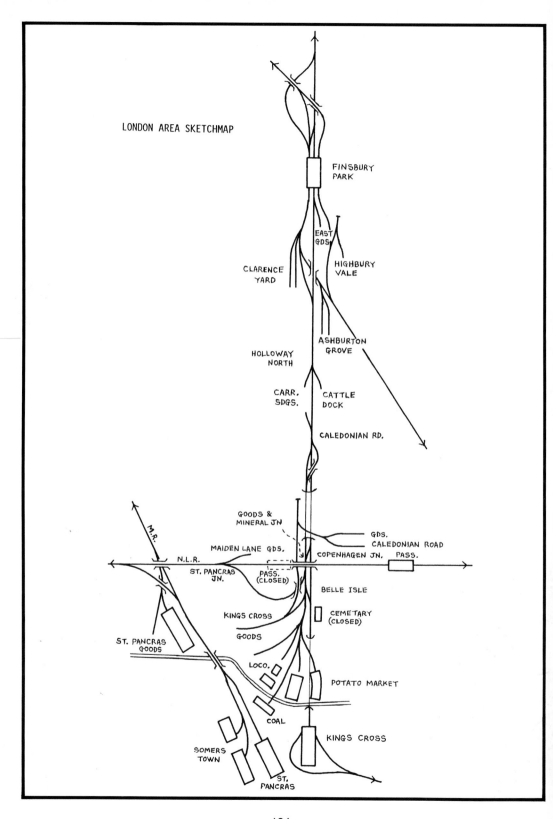

LONDON AREA SKETCHMAP

FINSBURY PARK

EAST GDS.

HIGHBURY VALE

CLARENCE YARD

ASHBURTON GROVE

HOLLOWAY NORTH

CARR. SDGS.

CATTLE DOCK

CALEDONIAN RD.

GOODS & MINERAL JN

GDS. CALEDONIAN ROAD PASS.

MAIDEN LANE GDS.

COPENHAGEN JN.

M.R.

N.L.R.

ST. PANCRAS JN.

PASS. (CLOSED)

BELLE ISLE

KINGS CROSS GOODS

CEMETARY (CLOSED)

ST. PANCRAS GOODS

LOCO.

POTATO MARKET

COAL

KINGS CROSS

SOMERS TOWN

ST. PANCRAS

acquired a still more democratic role when the British Broadcasting Corporation erected the metal mast which adorns its nearer end, and on 2 November 1936 commenced television transmissions. Here again, Britain has led the world; strictly speaking, the first television broadcast took place in Germany in October 1929, but it was a short-lived experiment, whereas the BBC service which started a few weeks later has continued since, apart from the war period. Many of today's 'Elizabethan' passengers will be sharing their firesides with familiar images ranging from 'Muffin the Mule' to 'Inspector Lockhart'.

Between Hornsey and Harringay stations lie the freight engine shed and the vast Ferme Park marshalling yard. Our driver steams to Finsbury Park, then shuts off and puts the brake on to slow to 35mph before the engine leaves the

Below:
Sir Ralph Wedgwood (originally *Herring Gull*) heading a marvellous selection of vintage vehicles, runs out of Copenhagen Tunnel on her way down into the terminus on 7 July 1947. Above the tunnel is the end of Frederica Street, where Ealing Film Studios built a sham house for their comedy feature film 'The Lady Killers'. The Killers disposed of their victims by dropping them into empty coal trains leaving King's Cross Goods.
E. R. Wethersett/IAL

seemingly endless tangle of yards and sidings to nose down into the black holes of Copenhagen Tunnel. Trains and engines are moving all over the place; among them we can identify the 4pm express for Cleethorpes coming through on the down fast line, the 3.54pm to Hatfield on the slow, the 4pm to Hertford hard on its heels, at least two down empty stock trains, the stock for the 5pm down rolling slowly through Finsbury Park, and the 'V2'-hauled 4.5pm King's Cross-York goods.

Emerging from Copenhagen Tunnel into the canyon of Belle Isle, we take a right turnout into the middle bore of Gasworks Tunnel, and here we brake her down to a jog-trot — a strict speed limit of 8mph applies to all movements on the King's Cross pointwork. Through the smoky darkness appear lamps on the wall, whose purpose is to tell you where you are and in which direction you are moving. The driver holds the brake on and, dead slow, the engine twists with slight uneasy jerks through the switches into Platform No 5. With just the straight empty line in front of him he puts the handle up momentarily until about half-way along, then pulls it down, the brakes enfold her and she stops five yards from the end. He drops the handle to the bottom of its travel, losing the last of the vacuum with a whoosh, turns off the small ejector and there is silence. It is 4.13pm; six hours, twenty-seven and a half minutes. No stops.

To Rest

Mallard still has some six feet to travel on her southward journey. A shunter steps down between the tracks on the left side of the engine, ducks between tender and leading coach to uncouple the vacuum hoses, stands up and utters the inarticulate shout by which all Londoners communicate. The driver blows his brake off, puts her in full gear, opens the regulator, shuts it and puts the brake in in one movement while the shunter yanks on the buckeye coupler chain; the engine draws clear and squeaks to a stop again.

In the cab the Haymarket men come up to chat while the drivers feel round the bearings and make out their tickets — the most important part of the day's work, without them we don't get paid and the managers have no fodder for their statistics. In the heart of the machine the great heat reservoir of the brick arch is slowly cooling down, still holding pressure at 240lb with the glass about two-thirds full. We have half an hour to stand here, so we may fill it with a glance round King's Cross station.

The twin arch roof under which we are standing is the original station, designed by Lewis Cubitt and opened in 1852 on what was then the edge of the city. The penurious GN was proud to report that the entire station cost less than the Euston propylaeum. Its weakness is that the offices are on the west side, and if you pass the screen wall at the inner end you are out in the street, an area that was meant to be a forecourt but is now filled with a meaningless clutter of huts. The eight platforms are numbered 1 to 10, with no 3 or 9. Platforms Nos 11 to 17, the suburban station, were added piecemeal and have the temporary look that all the GN timber-built stations achieve; No 16 being a steep incline on a connection off the Metropolitan line, termed either the Hotel Curve as it runs under the Great Northern Hotel, or more appositely the Drain. The corresponding up line goes past the separate platform called York Road. Opposite that is

Above left:
The 'Flying Scotsman' arriving in King's Cross. This was in 1953; the engine *Gannet* carries a Coronation emblem.
Ian Allan Library

Left:
At King's Cross on 26 July 1960, *Merlin* stands ready to take the 'Non-Stop' to Edinburgh.
Mrs A. Hatherill

Right:
We saw *Merlin* at Waverley on the up train, so here is a complementary view of her starting away from King's Cross Platform No 7 on 26 July 1960.
Mrs A Hatherill

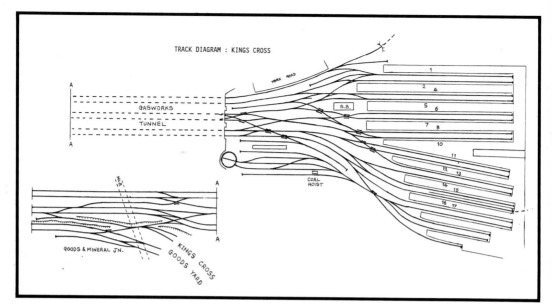

TRACK DIAGRAM : KINGS CROSS

a locomotive yard, called 'bottom shed' in distinction from 'top shed' up in the goods depot, built on the site of the former gas works that gave the tunnel its name. Operation is controlled by an all-electric power signalbox, equipped by the Siemens company, commissioned in 1932. Devotees of the 'Cross' hold the station in particular affection, perhaps by virtue of the English characteristic of pride in making oneself comfortable in a rather forbidding-looking place.

An 'N2' or an 'L1' 2-6-4T couples on to the far end of the 'Non-Stop' coaches and at 4.50pm sets off for Hornsey sidings. A junior driver and fireman from King's Cross No 7 Link arrive to take over *Mallard* from the main line crews who go off duty, and as soon as the coaches recede down the platform they follow them out to pull up at the end under the signalbox. A few minutes later a shunt signal changes and we run out into the tunnel, draw forward across the layout to a

Above:
After bringing up the 'Non-Stop', *Seagull* backing out past King's Cross box on 9 August 1959. The quantity of coal left in the tender is not as much as might be thought, for the bunker floor slopes upwards and most of what is visible is on a shelf at the back.
J. B. Bucknall

spur in the southwest corner, then back into the loco yard. With the evening rush just beginning, the convenience of this yard is apparent as it provides somewhere to park engines instead of having them cluttering up the crowded station approaches. While *Mallard* is in the yard a couple

Left:
It has been seen before, but no account featuring *Mallard* would be complete without this view of her standing in King's Cross on the evening of 30 March 1963, after working the up 'White Rose' from Leeds. She was taken out of use four weeks later. Rising above the firebox area of the engine are three roof girders slightly different from all the rest, replacements for a section that was destroyed by a bomb in 1941.
R. F. Roberts

Right:
Great Northern 0-6-2Ts were the staple motive power around King's Cross for nearly 50 years; 'N2' No 69548 makes a vigorous start although not disturbing the driver's cigarette. Behind her on the left is a metal assembly which is the locomotive yard coal hoist.
Mrs A. Hatherill.

of labourers can make a start on filling the tender up with selected coal, Eventually, and it could be late in the evening, she is given a path out to 'top shed' and is taken on to the down slow line, the left-hand one of the six. The driver works her on very easy steam so as not to draw too much cold air into the firebox. Out of the tunnel we turn left on one of the inclines leading in to the higher level goods yard approaches, and pull up, now under the control of Goods & Mineral Junction

box. The road is reset, and chimney-first we enter the locomotive depot.

Here the first stop is on the turntable to turn; next to the coaling plant if necessary to complete the task of loading seven tons of coal; then to the ashpit. The engine is secured with regulator firmly shut, reverser in mid gear, cylinder cocks open and handbrake hard on. The driver exam-

nes her for visible defects and the fireman opens up the 'cod's mouth' at the front with a crank handle provided. They leave her there for artisans to tackle the task of extracting ash from ashpan and smokebox; meanwhile, a fitter walks over, ducks underneath her in the pit, reappears a couple of minutes later and goes off to the offices. The result of this visit appears on the

Left:
Getting at the smokebox for the routine task of mucking out the char is made that much more difficult by the casing. These views are at Bridgnorth, Severn Valley Railway. We are pleased to report that when running on this line, crew changes were made in the traditional manner.
Both SHA

Shedmaster's desk in the form of a grubby slip of paper bearing the legend '22 2¼'. That refers to the depth of oil in the middle connecting rod big-end oil cup on '22' — 60022 to you. If it is much less than the last time it was measured, she will be taken out of service and the bearing dismantled, to investigate the state of wear of the whitemetal bearing surface or just to replace a felt pad which conducts oil to it from the reservoir. If the level has not gone down appreciably, then *Mallard* will be moved on to a berth in the running shed or on the 'back pits' over on the north side of the depot, there to be examined, cleaned and prepared for the next day: off to Grantham, Leeds, Newcastle perhaps, or Non-Stop to Edinburgh.

Below:
When *Mallard* was refurbished for museum display she was paired with a non-corridor tender similar to the one she had in 1938. In this view are visible, beneath the cab, the drop grate lever angled downwards, and the horizontal shaft to the speed recorder.
K. J. C. Jackson